BLACK VOYAGE

BLACK VOYAGE

EYEWITNESS ACCOUNTS
OF THE ATLANTIC SLAVE TRADE

Edited by
THOMAS HOWARD

LITTLE, BROWN AND COMPANY
BOSTON   TORONTO

To P. B. Smith Jr.

LIBRARY OF CONGRESS CATALOG CARD NO. 78-150058

FIRST EDITION

T 05/71

Published simultaneously in Canada
by Little, Brown & Company (Canada) Limited

PRINTED IN THE UNITED STATES OF AMERICA

CONTENTS

CHRONOLOGY OF THE ATLANTIC SLAVE TRADE

1433–1888

1433	Portuguese sea captains round Cape Bojador for the first time, beginning a series of explorations of the West African coast.
1442	A Portuguese sea captain returns home with ten slaves from Rio de Oro.
1480's	The Portuguese build a fort on the Gold Coast of West Africa, begin establishing slave trading routes.
1492	Columbus discovers the New World, opening the way for discovery of vast areas for agriculture, settlements by European powers.
1501	The Spanish take the first African slaves to the Caribbean colonies to work mines. Indian population rapidly disappears as a result of warfare, enslavement, disease.
1562	Sir John Hawkins is the first Englishman to carry Negro slaves to the New World.
1565	Saint Augustine is founded on the coast of Florida; slaves are reported to be there from the start; they are believed to be the first in what is now the United States.

1618   King James of England authorizes a stock company to engage in the West African slave trade, but it proves unprofitable.

1619   A Dutch vessel arrives at Jamestown in North America with twenty African slaves, the first in an English colony in the New World.

1631   The second charter is granted for Guinea trade by the English crown, but it also fails.

1638   The *Desire*, first American-built vessel to carry slaves, leaves Salem with seventeen Pequot Indians who were sold as slaves in the West Indies. The ship returned with cargo which included Negro slaves.

1640's   Sugar cane is introduced as a money crop in the West Indies. Large labor demands are met with increased shipments of Negro slaves.

1641   Massachusetts enacts the "Body of Liberties" forbidding slavery except of war captives or those willingly selling themselves into slavery.

1645   The *Rainbow* leaves Boston on the first voyage by an American vessel to engage expressly in the Atlantic slave trade.

1652   Rhode Island bans slavery.

1672   The Royal African Company is given monopoly by the English throne to supply the West Indies with three thousand African slaves annually.

1688   Quakers at Philadelphia issue a protest against slavery.

1698   The English crown throws open the slave trade to independent shipping firms.

1701–1714   The War of Spanish Succession, which sharply reduced the influence of Spain and Portugal in the African trade.

1713   The Asiento, reached at the Treaty of Utrecht, gives England the privilege of shipping forty-eight hundred slaves annually to Spanish colonies in the West Indies.

1740   The Virginia House of Burgesses adopts a law against the slave trade.

1739–1748	The War of Jenkins's Ear. Captain Robert Jenkins, an English merchant captain, is caught smuggling goods to the Spanish West Indies and his ear is cut off as an exemplary measure. It was one of many such incidents, but England uses it as provocation for war. Spanish influence is further reduced in the Atlantic trade.
1750	End of the Asiento.
1755–1763	The Seven Years War, between England and France, leads to the further ascendancy of the English in the African–New World trade.
1772	In a famous case brought by Granville Sharp, Lord Chief Justice Mansfield of Great Britain rules that when a slave sets foot on English soil he becomes free; the decision thus abolishes slavery in England.
1787	The Society for the Abolition of the Slave Trade is founded by Granville Sharp, Thomas Clarkson, pottery maker Josiah Wedgwood, and others. Sierra Leone is acquired for the settlement of freed slaves and is made a separate British colony in 1799.
1788	The British crown appoints a committee of the Privy Council to investigate English participation in the slave trade. Société des Amis des Noirs is formed in Paris to promote the abolition of slavery and slave trade.
1789	William Wilberforce, who championed the abolitionist cause in Parliament, opens his campaign in the House of Commons to end the slave trade. He succeeds in 1807.
1792	The cotton gin is invented, thus revolutionizing cotton agriculture, which spread rapidly across the Southern United States. By 1802 the slave trade is banned by Denmark, the first European power to take such a step.
1807	Slave trading by English vessels is banned by Parliament.
1808	The United States bans African slave trade.

1812	War of 1812, partially caused by British attempts to search U.S. merchant vessels.
1820	The Missouri Compromise, admitting Missouri as a slave state and Maine as a free state. But the debate raised the slavery question, which had been quiescent for years; it was to trouble the nation until the Civil War brought slavery to an end.
1822	Liberia founded as a colony for freed American slaves. Republic of Liberia founded in 1847.
1833	All slaves in British colonies emancipated.
1839	The *Amistad* mutiny, raising the question of the right of slaves to fight for their own freedom.
1841	The *Creole* incident.
1845	The *Felicidade* incident. British sailors taking a captured slave vessel back to port are slain by the vessel's crew. A British court rules for the crew because slaves were not found on board, just slaving equipment. But the decision serves to revive attempts to stop the trade.
1848	The French abolish slavery in their colonies.
1861–1865	The American Civil War, which effectively ended the African–New World slave trade. The Thirteenth Amendment is ratified in 1865, abolishing slavery in the United States, following President Lincoln's Emancipation Proclamation in 1863.
1888	Brazil frees its slaves, the last to be emancipated in the Western Hemisphere.

BLACK VOYAGE

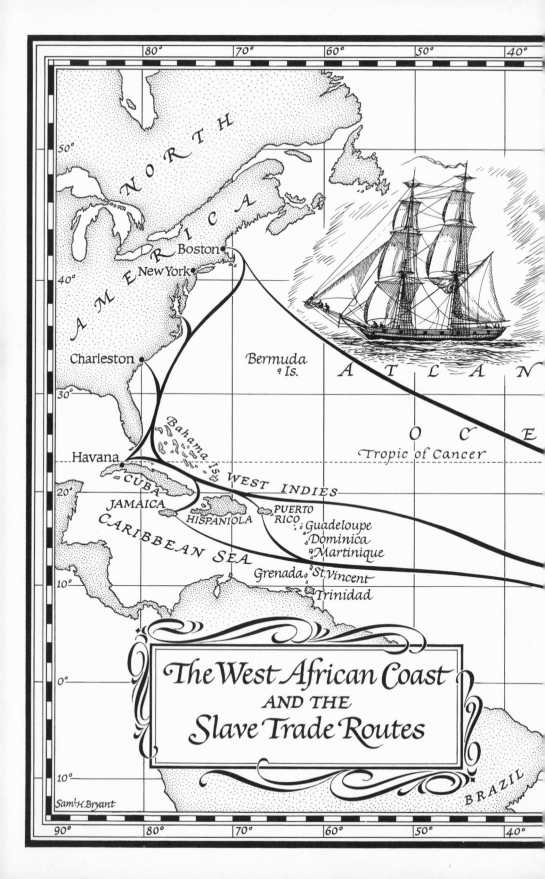

The West African Coast
AND THE
Slave Trade Routes

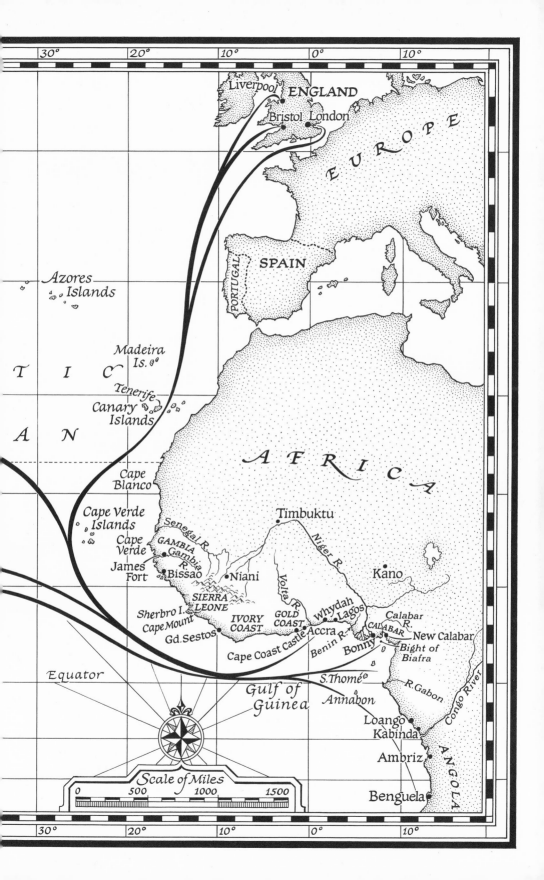

INTRODUCTION

A BRIEF HISTORY OF THE ATLANTIC SLAVE TRADE

Until just a few decades ago a voyage across the Atlantic Ocean was an experience of suffering and peril for passenger and crew alike. One historian, thinking of the immense loss of life, especially among those who traveled to work the new lands in the early years of the western Atlantic colonies, conjectured that if the sea could be drained between Europe and Africa and the New World, the paths of the ships would be easily traced by the bones of those who died in the ocean crossing. By far the clearest trace of these old searoads would likely be found along the route of the slave ships from Africa's west coast to the West Indies.

There is no accurate count of the number of African black men who made that fearful journey in chains, but it was in the millions. By assessing the records of various slave shipping firms, the head fees paid to port officials in the New World and similar documentary evidence, historians believe that from 10 to 20 million slaves were brought westward across the Atlantic during the four centuries the trade prevailed. And it is estimated that as many as one third — from 3.3 million to nearly 7 million —

never completed the trip. They died in bondage aboard ship and were thrown overboard.

From the fifteenth century, when this wellspring of flesh on Africa's western shores was first tapped, to a century ago when it was finally capped, the flow of slaves ran strong. Slaves were nearly always cheap in Africa and dear in the Caribbean islands. A captain could afford to pack his holds with black men and women, like so many spoons. He knew a certain number would die but that the price the rest would bring would more than make up for the loss of the dead.

As with the purchase, transport and sale of any commodity, economic gain was the prime reason for the trade from its beginning to its end. The New World needed labor and plenty of it, especially in the hot climes of the Caribbean. After Europeans had started settlements in the newly discovered lands across the Atlantic, they soon found that they were physically incapable of profitably working the soil in the tropical islands. The native Indians likewise were unable to do the arduous forced labor which the Europeans demanded. They died by the thousand in their unaccustomed bondage, or, seeing no reason to give up their independence to the white invader, they ran away. This proved a troublesome trait with which the Europeans found it difficult to cope since the Indians could take refuge in the forests they had grown up in.

Only a few years before the discovery of the New World, European venturers had discovered the west coast of Africa. On lands facing the Gulf of Guinea they found a country teeming with people. At first, the white men who wanted slaves sought to seize those blacks they wanted. Of course the blacks fought back or retreated into the forests. Then the Europeans discovered that there were Africans who were not averse to selling other Africans as slaves. Primitive tribal society existed in many areas of the continent, and many a victorious tribal chief willingly sold away the captives of a defeated tribe — glad enough to rid himself of future troubles.

The Negro soon was found particularly able to withstand the backbreaking field labor on the New World plantations — for a while at least. And when he buckled, a replacement could be had cheaply enough.

Through the four centuries of the trade, horror was compounded upon horror for the Africans who were herded to the rivers and shores and put aboard the slave ships. The black man caught up in the man traffic knew nothing but despair and physical misery. The swirl of this commerce reached into every corner and crevice of his continent and the curse was visited upon every tribe in some manner or another. Slave caravans traveled every trail that laced the vast land together, and the coffles* of ebony flesh wound ultimately to slave pens beside one sea or another.

Slave trading existed across the Red Sea and Indian Ocean both before and after the trade across the Atlantic, and there is some evidence that it still persists in the Arab strongholds east of the Red Sea. These eastern trade routes were almost always in the hands of Asians, and Europeans were little involved. Because the impact of the trade was greatest on the Western world, the East African trade is not considered here.

Nearly all European nations were involved in the Atlantic slave trade at one time or another. Those that abstained or that participated in a minor way did so only because they were muscled out by stronger powers. The European viewed the Negro he bought and sold as no better than a beast of burden, just as well-off in America as Africa. Few had any qualms about the trade until the last years of the eighteenth century. The defenders of the trade cited the Bible as approving slavery which would be beneficial for heathens. The zealots went so far to ease their consciences as to declare their slaving efforts to be evangelical be-

* Men fastened together in a chain.

cause they first baptized their slaves Christians before shipping
them across the ocean.

HOW AFRICANS WERE ENSLAVED

As noted above, the first slaves taken by Europeans were captured in quick raids on coastal villages. These actions brought
reprisals and resistance, however, and the next time Europeans
paid a call, they had disappointing returns. The raids were
soon discouraged, and the slavers made peace with tribal chieftains. The Europeans found the coastal chieftains anxious to
avoid raids on their own people and thus ready to fill the slave
ships with their enemies — for a price. Thus the trade took on
the rudiments of organization. The Europeans built castles and
forts along the coast to make up a network of trading stations to
collect and keep the slaves for the ships of nations engaged in the
trade. There is little dispute, however, that the lines of supply of
slaves from the interior slave markets remained predominantly
in the hands of black traders and chieftains throughout four
centuries. Africa was not the "Dark Continent" Europeans
blithely believed, but had its own businessmen who had innate
acumen in financial matters. These men preferred from the start
that white men stay on the coast while they managed the commerce inland. There were, of course, white men who trekked in
and out of Africa's slave merchandising centers, but there is little
evidence that what business lines they established survived their
deaths.

As the trade from the west coast developed, so did the supply
lines and the methods of enslavement. The normal population in
the lands immediately surrounding the western shores was not
enough to supply the ever increasing demands of the European
slave ships. Tribal wars had traditionally provided prisoners for
the victors and those captives the victors didn't want, they had
slain. But when the white men came to bargain, the chiefs began

selling the unwanted prisoners to be carried off forever, thus answering the same purpose of eliminating their enemies. The Europeans were not hesitant in using this practice for their own ends and encouraging tribal wars to promote a supply of new slaves.

The tribal chiefs also had the power, frequently exercised, to sell individual tribesmen into slavery for punishment of a real or trumped-up crime. Many husbands accused their wives of adultery to be rid of them in order to acquire others. Impoverished families sold their children to either buy food if their crops failed, or to reestablish themselves when hard times came. Kidnapping also was a widespread practice of native gangs who sought to fill slave coffles.

Europeans defended the practices used in enslaving Africans by arguing that they provided a reprieve for persons who would either have been slain as losers in tribal conflicts or punished in a land that lived by harsh rules. The white men maintained they were drawing off an excess population which would have starved anyway in a land that seemed to teem with a surplus of black bodies.

THE STATE OF AFRICAN CULTURE DURING
THE SLAVE TRADE

From its discovery, Africa was depicted as a continent of savages engaged in constant bloodletting and cannibalism that shocked European morals. The image that the average European had drawn for him of the African continent generally omitted any distinction between one area and its people and those of another. The white man rarely thought of Africa as being inhabited by anyone other than bloodthirsty savages from one end to the other. The image, which prevails even today, was patently untrue, and the high state of cultural development among the tribes attests to this. That horrible human sacrifices in the hundreds, and some said in the thousands, did occur in regions of Dahomey probably occurred as witnesses said. But the temperament of these ferocious people was in striking contrast to the hospitable, agrarian-oriented people who lived tranquil lives elsewhere. This book is not intended to elaborate on this point, but to note that at the time the following eyewitness accounts were written there was virtually no thought or consideration given to revising the traditional view of Africa.

West African cultures reached high levels of development in certain areas, as did other cultures in different parts of the continent. Some tribes had a distinct architecture and forms of republican government. Agriculture and husbandry had been well developed and complex economic and legal systems were in existence.

But there were obvious gaps. There was no written language to speak of and the technology of many tribes was little beyond that of the Iron Age. There was a wide diversity of spoken languages and the hundreds of dialects made it difficult for tribes, even of the same region, to communicate freely. Invaders, of whatever color, found it easy to divide them and set one tribe against another. The refusal of tribes to join in a common cause except under force was an important factor leading to their enslavement. This disunity has lasted through the years and is still one of the foremost concerns of thinking African statesmen who today are seeking to unite their continent.

WHERE THE SLAVES WERE CAPTURED

Although hardly a port in all of Africa escaped the visit of a slave ship at some point in history, the bulk of the slaves shipped in the Atlantic trade came from the Guinea Coast, described generally as that stretch from Cape Verde, Africa's westernmost tip, southward and around to the Congo. As the coastline became better known, ship captains named certain sections for the commodities likely to be traded there, such as the Grain Coast, in the vicinity of what is now Liberia; the Ivory Coast, immediately to the east; the Gold Coast; and the Slave Coast, now made up of the nations of Dahomey, Togo and Nigeria.

The thousands of miles of coastline facing the Gulf of Guinea are characterized by low-lying sandy beaches broken by small sluggish rivers that seep from jungles and swamps. The mouths of the rivers are blocked partially by treacherous sandbars where many ships met their end. There are few good harbors anywhere along the coast.

The climate was insufferably humid and unsuited for Europeans. It was no idle observation that the Guinea Coast was "the white man's grave." Most of the men who manned the slave factories* and trading settlements were the outcasts or the destitute of Europe. Few ever left the coast alive. The story of one such trader, identified only as Nics. Owen, is given later to show something of the embittered loneliness which he experienced in a life he could not escape, despite his longings to return home a rich man.

Explorations inland were rare, and most were disastrous. Transportation in the interior until recent years never progressed beyond a canoe on a steaming shallow river filled with alligators, or a swinging hammock borne by porters along the foot trails that crisscrossed the country. White men tended to stay on the coast. There they tried to live as they had lived in Europe. They often ate heavy foods and drank too much liquor in the sweltering climate. Far from home and in a primitive place, the white man, according to one visitor to the Guinea Coast in the late eighteenth century, "indulged every human passion with utter freedom, whether it be confirmed drunkenness or unrestrained intercourse

* A station where slaves were brought for trade. The station agent was called a factor.

with Negro girls. They knew that the deadly climate was likely to claim them eventually."

THE START OF THE ATLANTIC TRADE

The beginning of the slave trade across the Atlantic is generally dated from about 1433 when Prince Henry the Navigator, the Portuguese monarch, sent his sea captains venturing down the African coast. Until these explorations, seamen had believed the ocean ended in a swirling abyss not far past Cape Bojador, on the coast just below the Canary Islands. The Portuguese sailed a little farther down the coast on each voyage until they finally passed the hot western desert sands of the Sahara and found a lush tropical country. In 1442, a Portuguese skipper brought back ten Negroes as slaves from the vicinity of Rio de Oro. Prince Henry actually discouraged the commerce in black flesh, but was unable to stop his captains from indulging in it for long. By the 1480's, the Portuguese had built a fort on the Gold Coast and established slave trading lines there.

By the time Columbus sailed across the Atlantic, Negro slaves were fairly common in Lisbon and some historians think Columbus carried several with him to the New World. The black man, though an enslaved participant, also accompanied Balboa, Cortez and other Spanish conquistadores into the uncharted lands of the Western Hemisphere. There were Negro slaves in Florida from the time of the founding of Saint Augustine in 1565. Their descendants were freed three centuries later with the Confederate surrender at Appomattox.

The first African Negroes to be imported as slaves specifically for colonial labor were brought to the Spanish colonies in the Caribbean about 1501 to work mines there when the Spaniards had been unsuccessful in forcing the Indians to work. The governor of the Spanish colonies at first banned Negro slave imports, but decimation of the Indians forced the Spanish court to lift the ban.

ENGLAND RULES THE WAVES, AND THE SLAVES

During the first two centuries of its existence Spain and Portugal were the dominant powers in the African slave trade. The need for labor in their colonies was acute and the Iberians pressed their fleets to keep control of both the supply lines and the New World markets. However, both nations were eclipsed eventually by the Dutch, French and English. Through wars on land and sea and political manipulations in the royal courts, the trade was shifted back and forth as a highly valuable stake. European royalty and their merchant minions readily engaged in slave trading and enjoyed high profits from it. The Danes, Swedes and almost every other European nation took some part in the trade at one time or another. The War of the Spanish Succession in the opening years of the eighteenth century, however, ended with the influence of Spanish and Portuguese rulers sharply reduced and with England ascendant as the major power on the African coast from Gambia to the Congo. With the Asiento Agreement in 1713, England gained the privilege of supplying Spanish Caribbean colonies with forty-eight hundred slaves a year.

Sir John Hawkins, England's maritime hero of Elizabeth's reign, had the dubious honor of being the first Englishman to take Negro slaves to the New World. He sailed in 1562 on the first of three slaving voyages, obtained three hundred Negro slaves from the west coast of Africa and took them to the Spanish New World settlements where they were traded for hides, sugar, ginger and pearl. A second voyage was also successful, but the third ended as a disaster in an encounter with a Spanish fleet on the coast of Central America. Hawkins barely made it back to England with a battered remnant of his own fleet. After that the

English did not seriously contend for a share in the trade for approximately a century.

In the seventeenth century when the English did muscle their way into the slave trade, it remained in the king's hands to grant ship charters for such voyages. King James I authorized a group of London merchants to form a stock company for the Guinea trade in 1618, but it proved an unprofitable undertaking, and the charter was allowed to lapse. In 1631, a second monopoly for slave trading was granted by the English crown, but it likewise was never a robust enterprise. The Royal African Company was chartered in 1662 to supply the West Indies with three thousand Negroes annually but stiff competition from privately owned ships kept profits low, and in 1698 the crown allowed the trade to be thrown open for all.

By the time of the Asiento, the slave trade was the foundation of colonial commerce in the New World. During the century following, the slave traffic across the Atlantic swelled to a flood. It is estimated that from forty thousand to one hundred thousand slaves a year were transported to the New World during this hundred years, the annual volume varying with international conditions.

The English perfected a three-cornered trade. They shipped manufactured goods to the African coast to be traded for slaves. The slaves were then transported in the "middle passage," or second leg of the voyage, and the profits from their sale in the West Indies were taken in molasses or other West Indian products for the English market. Sugar cane, introduced into the Caribbean in the 1640's, proved to be a highly profitable crop. Huge rum distilleries were built in England to process the molasses into liquor for the thirsty populace.

The cane plantations required armies of laborers, and Negro slaves were considered the best, if not the only, means of providing manpower economically. In terms of cost and upkeep and work that could be forced from them in the few years they could be counted on to survive the harsh cane-field tasks, the Negroes were an economic boon. Many West Indian islands, where large plantations were first developed, became little more than armed prison camps where thousands of slave inmates lived under the most brutal working conditions. The demand for new slaves was heavy. The mortality rate of the slaves was high, and birth rates were far below what would have been sufficient to keep the slave population constant. The planters found it was cheaper to buy a new slave than raise one.

BEGINNING OF THE END

At the start of the eighteenth century, the Englishman was enjoying a new age of prosperity and his conscience was not easily pricked by the slave trade. The crown and the church condoned it, he argued. Slave ships often received the blessings of the local vicar as they set out on the ebb tides for the Guinea Coast. The slave trade was something that was remote from the greater part of the populace, who heard little of its horrors and saw only its rewards. Life for the English commoner was itself a grim struggle and left little time to pity anyone else. But as the industrial revolution improved living conditions, disturbing thoughts crept into the intellectual body of the nation. Tales of the grim conditions aboard slave ships became more widespread. A deep-rooted sense of justice and fair play grew to a surge of humanitarianism. Parliamentary restrictions on slave ships, aimed at improving the lot of the slaves carried aboard them, were put into effect. Finally, in 1807, the English slave trade itself was ended. Other nations took similar actions about the same time, but because England controlled the largest part of the trade, her course was by far the most significant. The crowning efforts of the abolitionist movement came in 1833 when slaves in all British colonies were emancipated.

The end of English participation in the slave trade and of slavery in her dominions came after a prolonged clash between the abolitionists and the political and economic forces supporting the trade. This clash was far more peaceful, however, than the one that occurred in North America. Here the roots of slavery were chopped out by the fratricidal Civil War, the greatest bloodshed in the history of the Western Hemisphere.

AMERICAN PARTICIPATION

The first slaves in the English colonies of North America were landed in 1619 by a Dutch vessel at Jamestown Island in Virginia. But, notwithstanding the scarcity of labor, slaves were not popular with the English colonists, and the number of slaves grew slowly. The English settlers had a ready supply of indentured servants or bond slaves — white men and women who could be treated with almost the same lack of regard as blacks until their terms expired. If the owner used proper foresight, he could extend the indentured servant's original contract for years in punishment for certain infractions. Bond slaves also were better than black slaves because they were already "seasoned," they knew their "place," were educated and there was no barrier of language to overcome.

White men, however, proved a problem in bondage. As a group they did not have the stamina to withstand the hard field work at the same low cost of maintenance as Negroes. And the white man cherished his independence too much. When his term expired, he left the plantations and pushed westward in search of his own land, and freedom from the oppression of the wealthy landowners back on the coast. Black slaves who loved their freedom none the less, did not have the privilege of a contract which would end after a certain number of years of work. They, and their children, were bought for life. In an alien world, they had to make the best of it.

The *Rainbow*, a New England-built ship, left Boston in 1645 for the first voyage by an American vessel to Africa expressly to engage in the slave trade. New England ports in the next two centuries were to vie vigorously with British merchants for slave shipping.

The New England colonies themselves never proved adaptable for the large slave holdings which were found to be more profitable on Southern plantations. Slaves were owned in New England and the other Northern colonies, but they never became an economic factor as they did in the South. The best markets for slaves were always in the Southern regions of North America. The New England shippers readily took to the triangular trade, shipping rum to Africa for slaves to be carried to the West Indies or the South, there to be swapped for cargoes of molasses, to make rum, or for rice or cotton. Until the American Revolution, almost all Negroes were taken to the West Indies first, then transshipped in smaller vessels to the mainland.

The American colonies gave birth to their own corps of zealots devoted to the cause of abolition of the slave trade. Many of the colonies were populated by fiercely independent men who had come to escape European tyrannies and shared no sympathy for the slaveholders. Quakers and Mennonites in the central colonies strongly opposed it and kept slavery from growing around them. Many Northerners and Southerners found slavery repugnant and freed their slaves. On January 1, 1808, the United States prohibited its citizens from taking part in the African slave commerce, although slavery as such in Southern states was not banned. It was of too much importance economically to the young nation and could not easily be stopped.

SLAVE SMUGGLING

The mere banning of the trade by the English and Americans, and other Atlantic nations could not bring it to a halt. When the door closed on legitimately chartered slave ships, an invitation was opened to smugglers of all nations to take part in the trade. Britain and other European nations launched sea patrols to halt the contraband slave traffic, but bringing an end to the trade was far from easy. As the legal supply of slaves came to a halt, the price of slaves in the West Indies and other western Atlantic slave markets went up, and the illegal supply rose to a flood to take economic advantage of the situation. Corruption among island officials was rife. There were too many coasts to watch, the seas were too wide, the landing places too many for the little squadrons to stop the torrent.

The United States gave token agreement to help stop the illegal activity, but it supplied only a small fleet of ships, most commanded by Southern officers who often looked the other way when a slave ship flying an American flag was overtaken. Congress, dominated by Southern senators and representatives, refused to allocate more than a nominal sum for the U.S. African squadron.

As could be expected, the American registry soon became popular with slave ship owners, who hired American captains and mates to command crews that were almost all foreign-born. The United States was steadfast in its refusal to permit British warships the right to stop and search American flag vessels for slaves. The refusal was a point of pride with the new nation, which felt that yielding on this point would only invite renewed bullying by the British lion. American statesmen argued vehemently that the British would use the right to search for slaves to bar legitimate American merchant vessels seeking to do honest trade anywhere on the African coast or in the West Indies. The

Americans had not many years before shucked off the British yoke, and they had little reason to trust the British. These very issues — violations of the flag on the high seas, confiscation of ships, illegal impressment — helped precipitate the war of 1812 with the British. Although there were many in United States officialdom anxious to stop the abuse of the American flag in the slave traffic, the tiny nation could ill afford the division that threatened.

It was not until the Webster–Ashburton Treaty of 1842 that the United States agreed to strengthen its African squadron and undertake its share of patrolling. The combined efforts of the Atlantic nations opposing the trade finally became effective and one by one the slave pens on the African coast were closed. It remained, however, for the American Civil War to completely throttle the trade to North America.

The Atlantic trade continued undercover south of the equator until at least 1888 when Brazil freed its slaves. They were the last to be emancipated in the Western Hemisphere.

There is evidence, attested to by news reports and stories of eyewitnesses filed with the United Nations and the British Parliament, that the slave trade continues today off the east coast of Africa. Slave coffles, though not the size they were a half century ago, make way under cover of night along little known trails of the Eastern countries. On reaching the coast, the slaves are loaded in swift dhows and whisked across the Red Sea and Indian Ocean to the Arabian Peninsula. The governments of the countries through which the slave traffic flows offer official denials, but testimonies and occasional arrests refute them.

The following eyewitness stories of persons who were actually involved in the Atlantic slave trade leave no doubt that the slave's voyage to the Western world was a trauma that will exist forever in the memory of mankind. It was a voyage conceived for greed, conducted by criminal violation, and its destination was devoid of hope for its passengers.

Historically it can be seen that the African slave trade flourished at a time when suffering and privation were the common lot of all men but a privileged few. The price of human life was small and the human dignities and freedom now found in the enlightened nations of the Western world simply did not exist two and three centuries ago. The following narrations depict one of the lowest levels reached by Western man, but it can be said that in his avarice Western man built a new set of nations in the New World where new concepts were given birth in a political and social climate that was nonexistent in the Old World. These narrations, penned by men who witnessed the horrors described, may show something of the raw molding of the forces that are still surging throughout the entire Western Hemisphere.

1

THE VOICE OF THE SLAVE

"THE FIRST OBJECT which saluted my eyes when I arrived on the coast was the sea and a slave ship which was then riding at anchor and waiting for its cargo. These filled me with astonishment, which was soon converted into terror when I was carried aboard. I was immediately handled and tossed up to see if I were sound by some of the crew; and I was now persuaded that I had gotten into a world of bad spirits and they were going to kill me."

The frightened slave was Olaudah Equiano, who was at the time only eleven years old. The year was 1756 and the slave ship was an English vessel on a slaving voyage to the Guinea Coast of Africa. Of the millions of African slaves taken from that continent during the four centuries of the slave trade to the New World, only a handful left accounts of their voyages across the Atlantic. Equiano was one of these, and he wrote one of the best descriptions of how it felt to be a slave. His account is also one of the few in English.*

In his memoirs, written after he won his freedom, Equiano describes his terror as a slave and the frustration and the suffer-

* Olaudah Equiano, *The Life of Olaudah Equiano, or Gustavus Vassa, the African*. Boston, 1837.

ing he and his countrymen felt. His writing echoes the deep anguish of the legions of his race who were caught up in the mesh of the man-trading commerce.

Equiano, who was later given the Christian name of Gustavus Vassa by an English owner, was born the son of a tribal chief in the interior of Nigeria about 1745. Until his arrival on the coast, Equiano had never seen or heard of the sea, or white men. By his own description, his countrymen were peaceful farmers, noted for their industriousness, intelligence and hardiness — qualities which unfortunately made them attractive as slaves. He and a younger sister were kidnapped from their home by two strangers who staged a quick raid while the adults of the village were working in the fields nearby. Equiano was separated from his sister several days later and saw her only once after that, for one brief moment when their slave coffles chanced to pass each other on an African trail.

He was sold first to a smith to work the bellows. He escaped, was caught and sold again. The youngster was then taken to a slave market in a town somewhere in Central Africa and there put in a slave coffle bound for the coast of Guinea. It reached its destination after weeks of traveling on foot or in log canoes.

In his autobiography, Equiano tells of his first moments aboard the slave ship. Ironically, he expected to be slain and eaten by the crew, whom he mistook for a group of savages.

"Their complexions, differing so much from ours, their long hair and the language they spoke, which was different from any I had ever heard, united to confirm me in this belief. Indeed, such were the horrors of my views and fears at the moment, that if ten thousand worlds had been my own, I would have freely parted with them all to have exchanged my condition with that of the meanest slave of my own country. When I looked around the ship and saw a large furnace of copper boiling, and a multitude of black people of every description chained together, every one of their countenances expressing dejection and sorrow, I no longer doubted my fate. Quite overpowered with horror and anguish, I fell motionless on the deck and fainted. When I recovered a little, I found some black people about me, and I believe some were those who had brought me on board and had been receiving their pay. They talked to me in order to cheer me up, but all in vain. I asked them if we were not to be eaten by those white men with horrible looks, red faces and long hair. They told me I was not."

A member of the crew sought to aid the terrified child and brought him a glass of rum, but Equiano refused to accept it until the sailor handed it first to one of the native traders who in turn handed it to the boy.

"I took a little down my palate, which, instead of reviving me as they thought it would, threw me into the greatest consternation at the strange feeling it produced, having never tasted such liquor before. Soon after this, the blacks who had brought me on board went off and left me abandoned to despair."

Completely alone in a nightmare world of heaving decks and creaking spars, the boy was in the depths of misery. "I now saw myself deprived of all chance of returning to my native country or even the least glimpse of hope of gaining the shore, which I now considered as friendly. I even wished for my former slavery in preference to my present situation, which was filled with horrors of every kind . . ."

His suffering had only begun. Soon afterwards, he was led to a grated hatchway and ordered into the cargo hold, already filled with slaves bought before him.

"There I received such a salutation in my nostrils as I had never experienced in my life. With the loathesomeness of the stench, and the crying together, I became so sick and low that I was not able to eat, nor had I the least desire to taste anything. I now wished for the last friend, Death, to relieve me."

But his captors had methods to change his mind.

"Soon, to my grief, two of the white men offered me eatables and on my refusing to eat, one of them held me fast by the hands and laid me across the windlass and tied my feet while the other flogged me severely. I had never experienced anything of this kind before. If I could have gotten over the nettings, I would have jumped over the side, but I could not. The crew used to watch very closely those of us who were not chained down to the decks, lest we should leap into the water. I have seen some of these poor African prisoners most severely cut for attempting to do so, and hourly whipped for not eating. This indeed was often the case with myself."

In a little while, he found some of his own tribe among the other slaves, and their companionship began to ease his extreme distress.

"I inquired of these what was to be done with us. They gave me to understand we were to be carried to these white people's country to work for them. I then was a little revived, and thought if it were no worse than working, my situation was not so desperate. But still I feared that I should be put to death, the white people looked and acted in so savage a manner. I have never seen among my people such instances of brutal cruelty, and this not only shown towards us blacks, but also to some of the whites themselves."

Coming from a slave the following comment on the callous attitude that prevailed among masters toward their crews is particularly poignant.

"One white man in particular I saw, when we were permitted to be on deck, flogged so unmercifully with a large rope near the foremast that he died in consequence of it, and they tossed him over the side as they would have done a brute. This made me fear these people the more, and I expected nothing less than to be treated in the same manner."

But the youngster gradually overcame his fright and began to ply his friends and fellow slaves with more questions about the mysterious and harsh world into which he had suddenly been thrust.

"I asked them if these people had no country, but lived in this hollow place? They told me they did not but came from a distant land. 'Then,' said I, 'how comes it that in all our country we never heard of them?'

"They told me because they lived so very far off. I then asked where were their women? Had they any like themselves? I was told they had.

" 'And why do we not see them' I asked. They answered, 'Because they were left behind.'

"I asked how the vessel would go? They told me they could not tell, but there was cloth put upon the masts by the help of the ropes I saw, and then vessels went on, and the white men had some spell or magic they put in the water when they liked in order to stop the vessel when they liked.

"I was exceedingly amazed at this account, and really thought they were spirits. I therefore wished much to be from amongst them, for I expected they would sacrifice me. But my wishes were in vain — for we were so quartered that it was impossible for any of us to make our escape."

Equiano said that while they stayed on the coast he was allowed to stay on deck most of the time. One day, to their astonishment, another ship came with its sails up. The newly arrived vessel anchored nearby and when the slaves on deck saw it stop, they were convinced then that the white man's magic worked.

"At last, when the ship we were in had got in all her cargo, they made ready with many fearful noises, and we were all put under deck, so that we could not see how they managed the vessel." Thus at eleven, Equiano was departing his homeland, which, unlike the others on board, he was destined to see again.

For of the millions who were taken across the Atlantic in chains, Olaudah Equiano and only a very scant number of his fellow Africans ever had the privilege of returning. If Equiano's fortune was unique in its outcome, his departure and passage were no different from those other millions. His description of the voyage was of necessity written from the view of the hold, not the quarterdeck.

"The stench of the hold while we were on the coast was so intolerably loathsome, that it was dangerous to remain there for any time . . . some of us had been permitted to stay on the deck for the fresh air. But now that the whole ship's cargo were confined together, it became absolutely pestilential. The closeness of the place and the heat of the climate, added to the number of the ship, which was so crowded that each had scarcely room to turn himself, almost suffocated us.

"This produced copious perspirations so that the air became unfit for respiration from a variety of loathsome smells, and brought on a sickness among the slaves, of which many died — thus falling victims of the improvident avarice, as I may call it, of their purchasers. This wretched situation was again aggravated by the galling of the chains, which now became insupportable, and the filth of the necessary tubs [used for sanitary purposes] into which the children often fell and were almost suffocated. The shrieks of the women and the groans of the dying rendered the whole a scene of horror almost inconceivable.

"Happily perhaps for myself, I was soon reduced so low that it was necessary to keep me almost always on deck and from my extreme youth I was not put into fetters. In this situation I expected every hour to share the fate of my companions, some of whom were almost daily brought upon the deck at the point of death, which I began to hope would soon put an end to my miseries. Often did I think many of the inhabitants of the deep much more happy than myself. I envied them the freedom they enjoyed, and as often wished I could change my condition for theirs. Every circumstance I met with, served only to render my state more painful and heightened my apprehensions and my opinion of the cruelty of the whites."

The bitter young slave related one incident in which the disdain of the crew for their human cargo was openly expressed. The sailors caught a number of fish and after they had eaten all they wanted, they threw the rest back into the sea rather than give any to the tantalized slaves nearby.

"We begged and prayed for some as well as we could, but in vain. Some of my countrymen, being pressed for hunger, took an opportunity when they thought no one saw them, of trying to get some, a little privately, but they were discovered, and the attempt procured for them some very severe floggings."

The miserable conditions on ship wore heavily on the captives, draining them of their will to live. "One day, when we had a smooth sea and moderate wind, two of my wearied countrymen who were chained together (I was near them at the time), preferring death to such a life of misery, somehow made through the nettings and jumped into the sea. Immediately another quite dejected fellow, who on account of his illness was suffered to be out of irons, followed their example. I believe many more would very soon have done the same if they had not been prevented by the ship's crew, who were instantly alarmed. Those of us that were the most active were in a moment put down under the deck, and there was such a noise and confusion among the people of the ship as I never heard before to stop her and get the boat out to go after the slaves. However, two of the wretches were drowned, but they got the other and afterwards flogged him unmercifully for thus attempting to prefer death to slavery . . .

"I can now relate hardships which are inseparable from this accursed trade. Many a time we were near suffocation from the want of fresh air, which we were often without for whole days together. This, and the stench of the necessary tubs, carried off many."

Equiano said that toward the end of the long voyage as the ship moved into calmer waters, he was permitted to stay on deck more of the time. He watched the seamen use the ship's quadrant to plot their course, and he was given a peek through the instrument by a sailor who noticed the boy's curiosity. Equiano was enraptured.

"The clouds appeared to me to be land, which disappeared as they passed along. This heightened my wonder; and I was now more persuaded than ever I was in another world and that everything about me was magic."

After several months of sailing, the ship at last reached the island of Barbados, the easternmost landfall of the West Indies. The crew gave a great shout and made signs of joy to the slaves. The end of the dread middle passage was over both for crew and cargo. The crew of the ship still faced a long Atlantic voyage back to England, but the seamen looked forward to the prospects of pay and home at the end of their journey. For the slaves, the journey's end was near and would close with their sale into a lifetime of bondage.

"As the vessel drew nearer, we plainly saw the harbor and other ships of different kinds and sizes and we soon anchored amongst them off Bridgetown. Many merchants and planters came on board . . . They put us in separate parcels and examined us attentively. They also made us jump, and pointed to the land, signifying we were to go there. We thought by this we should be eaten by these ugly men, as they appeared to us. When soon after we were all put down under the deck again, there was much dread and trembling among us and nothing but bitter cries to be heard all the night from these apprehensions. At last the white people got some old slaves from the land to pacify us. They told us we were not to be eaten, but to work, and were soon to go on land, where we should see many of our country people. This report eased us much, and sure enough, soon after we landed, there came to us Africans of all languages."

Equiano described the port in this way: "We were conducted immediately to the merchant's yard, where we were all pent up together, like so many sheep in a fold, without regard to sex or age. As every object was new to me, everything I saw filled me with surprise. What struck me first was that the houses were built with bricks and stories, and in every respect different from those I had seen in Africa, but I was still more astonished to see people on horseback. I did not know what this could mean, and indeed I thought these people were full of nothing but magical arts. While I was in this astonishment, one of my fellow prisoners spoke to a countryman of his about the horses who said they were the same kind they had in their country. I understood them, though they were from a distant part of Africa and I thought it odd I had not seen any horses there; but afterwards when I came to converse with different Africans, I found they had many horses amongst them, and much larger than those I then saw.

"We were not many days in the merchant's custody, before we were sold after their usual manner . . . On a signal given, (as the beat of a drum), buyers rush at once into the yard where the slaves are confined, and make a choice of that parcel they like best. The noise and clamor with which this is attended, and the eagerness visible in the countenances of the buyers, serve not a little to increase the apprehension of terrified Africans . . . In this manner, without scruple, are relations and friends separated, most of them never to see each other again. [For another description of this "scramble" see Chapter 7.] I remember in the vessel in which I was brought over . . . there were several brothers who, in the sale, were sold in different lots; and it was very moving on this occasion, to see and hear their cries in parting."

At this point in his autobiography, Equiano halted to plead with his readers to hear him, an African and former slave, on the iniquity of separating men from their loved ones in this manner. He was writing at a time when the slave trade still persisted in strength, but the plaintive note still sounds across the centuries as a reminder of the depravity of slavery.

"Oh, ye nominal Christians. Might not an African ask you — learned you this from your God, who says unto you, Do unto all men as you would men should do unto you? Is it not enough that we are torn from our country and friends, to toil for your luxury and lust of gain? Must every tender feeling be likewise sacrificed to your avarice? Are the dearest friends and relations, now rendered more dear by their separation from their kindred, still to be parted from each other, and thus prevented from cheering the gloom of slavery, with the small comfort of being together, and mingling their sufferings and sorrows? Why are parents to lose their children, brothers their sisters or husbands their wives? Surely this is a new refinement of cruelty, which, while it has no advantage to atone for it, thus aggravates distress, and adds fresh horror to the wretchedness of slavery."

Equiano and several other slaves were not immediately purchased because of what he said was "very much fretting" on their part, but they were bought finally, and within a few days were shipped to North America. Equiano was eventually sold there to a Virginia plantation owner. He might have spent his life in Virginia, working and catering to the needs of the planter and his family, but Equiano's travels were not at an end.

Some months afterwards, the captain of a visiting English ship purchased him and took the young slave to England, renaming him Gustavus Vassa and turning him over to the care of his wife and, in time, other families nearby. His new masters treated him with more kindness than he had met since his capture. Equiano wrote that he was raised by the captain's wife and the other families along with their own children. However, after a few years the ship captain took Equiano with him to sea as his servant. The captain had become an officer in the Royal Navy, and he and the slave participated in a number of naval engagements against the French in one of the endless periods of hostilities between those two nations. While at sea this time, Equiano learned more English and was baptized a Christian. This baptism resulted in a sudden downturn in his fortunes. Persuaded by his shipmates that he could win his freedom under English law that would free a Christian, Equiano sought legal release from his bondage. But his master, willing to give the young slave a maximum of benefits but not his freedom, frowned on the scheme and immediately sent Equiano back to the West Indies and ordered him sold.

There Equiano was purchased by a Quaker merchant named Robert King, who treated the youth and his other slaves with humaneness. But this treatment was far from standard. Equiano witnessed many instances of cruelty and mistreatment of slaves owned by others and he described the bitter, bleak existence of the average slave of the West Indies in the 1760's.

"While I was thus employed by my master [King], I was often witness to cruelties of every kind which were exercised on my unhappy fellow slaves. I used frequently to have different cargoes of new Negroes in my care for sale; and it was almost a constant practice with our clerks and other whites to commit violent depradations on the chastity of the female slaves; and these I was, though with reluctance, obliged to submit to all the time, being unable to stop them.

"When we have had some of these slaves on board my master's vessels, to carry them to other islands, or to America, I have known the mates to commit these acts most shamefully, to the disgrace not only of Christians, but of men. I have even known them to gratify their brutal passion with females not ten years old.

"These abominations some of them practiced to such scandalous excess that one of our captains discharged the mate and others on that account. And yet in Montserrat, I have seen a Negro man staked to the ground and cut most shockingly and then his ears cut off bit by bit because he had been connected with a white woman who was a common prostitute. As if it were no crime in the whites to rob an innocent African girl of her virtue but most heinous of a black man only to gratify a passion of nature where the temptation was offered by one of a different color, though the most abandoned woman of her species."

Equiano related the dialogue he had with a white trader that further illustrated the paradox. "Once Mr. D [a white trader] told me that he sold 41,000 Negroes and that he once cut off a Negro man's leg for running away. I asked him if the man had died in the operation, how he, as a Christian, could answer for the horrid act before God? And he told me, answering was a thing of another world. What he thought and did were policy. I told him that the Christian doctrine taught us to do unto others as we would that others should do unto us. He then said that his scheme had the desired effect — it cured that man and some others of running away."

Equiano's attempts to reason undoubtedly left no dent in the planter's conscience. His view was certainly shared by most New World colonists of that day. Retribution was swift and harsh for the slave who violated the most minor rule imposed by a master, and it was extreme if the master's life was threatened.

"Another Negro man was half hanged," Equiano wrote, "and then burnt for attempting to poison a cruel overseer.

"Thus by repeated cruelties, are the wretched first urged to despair, and then murdered, because they still retain so much of human nature about them as to wish to put an end to their misery, and retaliate on their tyrants. These overseers are indeed for the most part persons of the worst character of any denomination of men in the West Indies. Unfortunately, many humane gentlemen, but not residing on their estates, are obliged to leave the management of them in the hands of these human butchers, who cut and mangle the slaves in a shocking manner on the most trifling occasions, and altogether treat them like brutes. They pay no regard to the situation of pregnant women, nor the least attention to the lodging of field Negroes . . . To the honor of humanity, I knew several gentlemen who managed their estates . . . and they found that benevolence was their true interest."

The oppressive living conditions resulted in a decline in birth rates among the slave population, a situation which required thousands of new slaves each year to "fill the vacant places of the dead."

It was customary for Negro field hands to gather grass bundles to sell in the marketplace for the pittances these would bring. "Nothing is more common than for the white people on this occasion to take the grass from them without paying for it. . . . Too often . . . to my knowledge, our clerks and many others at the same time have committed acts of violence on the poor, wretched and helpless females, whom I have seen for hours stand crying to no purpose and get no redress or pay of any kind."

Equiano angrily calls for heavenly justice for the plight of the slaves, and appears to try his own newfound Christian faith in so doing. "Is not this one common and crying sin enough to bring down God's judgment on these islands?" he asks. "He tells us the oppressor and the oppressed are both in his hands; and if these are not the poor, the broken-hearted, the blind, the captive, the bruised, which our Saviour speaks of, who are they?"

As an entrusted slave of the merchant, King, Equiano made

trips to other islands to buy and sell goods and once on a trip to St. Kitts he bought a Bible and studied it assiduously. Then, in 1766, King granted Equiano his freedom, at long last.

Equiano thanked his benefactor, left the West Indies and after undergoing a series of adventures, including shipwrecks and kidnapping, he eventually made his way back to England where he turned seriously to Christian study. In 1784, an English church commissioned him as a missionary and sent him back to his people in Africa. As was to be expected, he became a foe of the slave trade, joining with English abolitionists in an all-out attack on the commerce.

Equiano maintained steadfastly in his memoirs that the slave trade degraded all men involved in it, owner and slave alike. "In all the different islands I have been (and I have visited no less than fifteen), the treatment of the slaves was nearly the same; so nearly, indeed, that the history of an island, or even a plantation, with a few such exceptions . . . might serve as a history of the whole. Such a tendency has the slave trade to debauch men's minds, and harden them to every feeling of humanity. I will not suppose that dealers in slaves were born worse than other men. No, such is the fatality of this mistaken avarice, that it corrupts the milk of human kindness and turns it into gall. Had the pursuits of those men been different, they might have been as generous, as tender-hearted and just, as they are unfeeling, rapacious and cruel. Surely this traffic cannot be good, which spreads like a pestilence and taints what it touches. Which violates that first natural right of mankind, equality and independency, and gives one man a dominion over his fellows which God could never intend."

2

THE SLAVE TRADER

A PETULANT WHITE SLAVE TRADER on the coast of West Africa in the mid-eighteenth century wrote of his troubles in dealing with his black counterparts:

"You are obliged to treat them all to liquer before you purchase anything or not; at the same time you are liable to thier noise and bad language without any satisfaction. You are obliged to take all advantages and lave [leave] all bounds of justice when trading with these creatures as they do by you, otherwise your goods won't fetch their starting prices at home."*

The contempt of the trader for his fellow businessmen was born from the depravity of the commerce itself, and the tragic degradation of everyone who became involved. For good reason, Africa's west coast became known as the "white man's grave." Of the many who sought their fortunes there, few were successful. The rest wore themselves out in the torrid climates, fighting diseases they were unaccustomed to, coping with the intrinsic problems of a business they learned viciously fast or failed.

The author of the description above was not one of the successful. Instead, he probably was representative of those whites who

* Nics. Owen, *Journal of a Slave Dealer*. Edited by Evaline Martin. London, 1930.

struggled pathetically, frustrated by living in an inhospitable land, and who died, bitter and depressed. In his journal, which covers his last five years as a white trader on the Guinea Coast, he is identified only as Nics. Owen. Like many another trader, he was cast into the trade by personal misfortune and once there sought desperately to make a financial recovery so he could return home. He used his journal to assuage his failure.

Owen took the slave trade as he found it, a valued branch of the English commerce and one which he frankly admitted was a way "to enlarge my fortune by honest means." Nowhere in his journal does he express repugnance of the trade or show any concern for the inhumanity shown the slaves.

Owen and his brother, Blayney, had gone on a voyage to Africa; their ship was seized by Africans in reprisal for some grievance. Imprisoned, the two brothers were penniless and were rescued from captivity by a slave dealer named Richard Hall, who employed them as his agents at slave posts. Hall, a castoff like Owen, was also making the best of a life not his choosing. A doctor, he had been taken prisoner by Africans and held a captive for three years before being rescued. Owen writes of Hall:

"This gentleman was one who has, like a great many others, spent his estate at home, therefore [was] obliged to go abroad in search of a new one, one of these who goes by general name of a good fellow, that dispizes all, who shrinks his shoulders at that generous spirit of liberality, one who said in his heart 'Let tomorow provide for itself' and to conclude he had a good many principles of honour, yet mix't with some stains that make his charecter [dubious]."

Owen and his brother, having no means of leaving, settled in their new work as agents of Hall: Owen on Sherbro Island off Sierra Leone and Blayney at a station on the Jong River. Owen confides in his journal that he had trouble dealing with the native traders, upon whom he had to depend to supply him with slaves.

The Africans kept a tight rein on the inland slave traffic and the white coastal traders were compelled to purchase slaves from them. Owen, obviously vexed at the advantage they held, wrote:

"These people that go by the names of kings and princes are only so in title. Their substance consists of nothing more than a lace hat, a gown, and silver-headed cane and a mat to sit upon, which serves to distinguish them from the rest of the Negroes."

He mocked their religious practices.

"It seems strange that here in this country you'll find men of ready wit in all things relating to common busness, yet if they are question'd conserning a future state, they give up all pretentions to humanity and wander in absurdities as black as their faces. They laugh at one anothers misfortunes and don't seem to repine their own, given to drunkiness and quarreling, being very cowardly and great boasters, miserably poor in general and live low as to victuals, soon provoked to anger and soon made up again if the offender makes an acknowledgement of his crime or pays, otherwise it is never at an end."

Owen eventually moved to the trading post on the Jong River to join his brother when Blayney became ill. He describes his life as anything but pleasant.

"In this place I find several ugly things that's not common at York Island, such as long worms and frogs; the latter makes such horrid noises in the night that it breaks my sleep. Last night I found one of these worms eight or nine inches long under my bed, which was the ocasion of my not sleeping until 11 or 12 a clock.

"My diet is rice and fouls, sometimes salt provisions, palm and slabar sauce . . . When it can be had I use coffie, tea and chocolate, for we are seldom so happy as to have plentey of English provisions in this place. I live here, but not with so much strength as I was want in Europe or any cold climate; my bones seem weaker and in hot weather I am favourish [feverish].

What most troubles me is the musquetos, who hinder me from sleep at night, and in the day large flies supply their places, and are no less troublesome; the bite of one of these flyes is so penetrating that your shirt will hardly keep it out. The pain is worse after the bites than for the pressent."

His perspective was not dimmed though, because he still felt his new situation was an improvement on the life he led at sea.

"It is to be considered that in the life of a saylor there is some things to sweetin the hardships of a voyage, as the hopes of seeing strange countrys, the expectation of gain and lastly the joy of seeing your native country at your return. Indeed saylors are commonly mery, hartey people and wares [wear] out the difficultey of a voyage with patience, but upon their return lay out the fruts [fruits] of thier labour in debaucherys, without consideration of future wants. This I always found to be the charetar [character] of an English seaman in my long experance upon that element of eight or nine years, in which time I have had very little communication with my country or any place else, except the time of loading and dischargeing our ship in whatever place we ware consighned. I must say the life of a seaman is in no ways agreeable to a man of quiet disposition, but he that is wild and rakishly inclin'd, turbilant in manners and loves liquor and bad company, shall very often have the uper hand in a ship's crew . . .

"I think in my opinion that a saylor that has no other means to satisfy the nececereys of this life than sailing the sais [seas] for wages, I look upon him to be more miserable than a poor farmer who lives upon his labour, who can rest at night upon a bed of straw in obscurity, than a saylor who comforts himself in the main top by blowing of [on] his fingers on a frostey night."

When Owen considered the visitors to his station and recalled those men he had known as a seaman, it was the New Englanders who impressed him most.

"It very often happens in New England that if a man is es-teem'd for his honesty in publick, let him be of what profession so ever, he is to be prefer'd in a ship . . . There's a great many re-marks of simplisity laid to the charge of these people by Euro-pains, which I find no reason why they should not be commended rather than a matter of laughter, as they supply the places of swearing and imprecations, which our old Europains are too much in love with. However, all that can be laid to their charge can never dominish their well known charectar of an industuri-ous honest people, who dispizes the gaudey toys of the foolish for things more substansial and nececery for the life of man."

As can be seen, Owen's remarks in his journal yield far more insight into his own character and moods than any accurate pic-ture of the African coast. Writing of the impact of three hundred years of European civilization on that coast, Owen commented: "It seems to me that the blacks on this coast retain their ancient custums without alteration in any thing, except their cloathing, which alters a good deal by the help of Europain cloath. Swords and househould furneture, likewise have made some adition to thier granduer with our goods in general. As to our religon it has made no impression in the least otherwise than a matter of redicule or laughter in so many years as they have had us among them, notwithstanding there has been some trials to convert them to a notion of a better state."

In his last two years, Owen began to date his journal with more regularity, and his despondency becomes more and more evident.

May 27, 1757. "It has seldom know such a scarcety of shiping upon the coast as at the pressent time and such a bad time for trade; from Siera Lone to Cape Mount there [is] not above three or four sail of ships that come for trade." This, he said, was "of bad consequence to us that live in the country, depending upon quik returns of goods. The blacks are keeping up to their old price, let it be war or pace [peace] besides the great expences of our houses and kings, which is not much less than 50 crowns pr. month, one month with another, which is of great expense.

"As I am much inclin'd to be malloncoly [melancholy], this place so far suits with my inclineations that if it ware not for sertain domestic troubles I should think myself happy even in this miserable country, without ever thinking of Europe or its pleasures. From my window I can see all of the adjacent country with part of the River Sherbro and the king's town to the east, again to the west the sea lies open to your view, with the dreadfull waves that rools over the barr and shouls in the mouth of the river, which occations a murmuring noise even at the house where we live."

"July [1757] has past without anything meteral [material] saveing the great decay of trade in these parts occasioned by the French war and scarcity of English shiping, which has rendered the price of a slave 10 bars less than usual so that the common price aboard ship is 70 bars."

At this point, Owen gives a detailed description of a wealthy mulatto trader near him. "He commonly goes by the name of Henry Tucker and lives upon the same shoar as we do about a mile distant. He has been in England, Spain and Portugall and is master of the English tongue. He has six or seven wives and numerous offspring of suns and daughters. His strength consists of his own slaves and their children, who has built a town about him . . . This man bears the charectar of a fair trader among the Europains, but to the contrary among the blacks. His riches sets him above the kings and his numerous people above being surprized by war. Almost all the blacks ows him money, which bring a dread of being stopt upon that acount, so that he is esteem'd and feared by all who has the misfortune to be in his power. He's a fat man and fair spoken, and lives after the manner of the English, haveing his house well furnish'd with English goods and his table tolarably well furnish'd with the country produce. He dresses gayley and commonly makes [use] of silver at his table, having a good side board of plate."

The Seven Years War was under way and, despondently, Owen views his own plight: "It is terrible to consider our situation. If we go home we are liable to be taken by the Frensh. If we remain here we are surounded by the worst of people, who considers nothing but your abilites to do them service. When your money's gone, so is their friendship and assistance too. We are here only seven degrees from the line [the equator] and above 2,900 miles from our native seat, among a barbarous people that knows neither God or a good quality in man. Some people think it strange that we should stay so long among people of the above charetar, when we have so many opertuniteys of going of the coast home. But I say, Europe is certainly the garden of the world, yet there's very little groes there for a passing traveler for nothing. A man that has spent his prime abroad, notwithstanding all his misfortunes, as shipwrecks, plundering and a hundred other things that ocors in the life of a saylor, I say that these things will not keep him from the charectar of a proddigal sun, who has spent his time idely abroad.

"It's not every man's fortune to get money, tho' of the greatest capasity, yet them that's look't upon as dull wretches as to other affairs commonly has the greatest bank. Let a man be ever so deligent and have bad fortune, the commons of the world will never believe otherwise than it's oueing [owing] to his extravagences of some sort or other."

But a trader's life was still better than a sailor's, said Owen. "Some people may condemn this kind of life and prefer that of a venturious saylor, valliant soldier, but I can tell them to try both first and then take their choice."

In August 1757, Owen and his brother, Blayney, agree to separate to see if their declining trade could be improved. Despite his preference for the life of a trader, Owen must often have feared for his life.

November 1757. "There has been a most barbarous instance of the creuel nature of these wretched people nigh where I live two days ago." Several natives had seized a fellow countryman on a trail at night, then eaten him. Owen described the mode of cannibalism. "As soon as thier prize is secure they devour him without mercy along with their ascociates in the bushes, who has prapared a fire for that purpose." He said local laws prohibited cannibalism and the culprits were quickly captured, convicted, put to death and their bodies burned to ashes.

Treachery on the Guinea Coast was not unknown among Europeans and Owen tells of an incident between two captains who had been frequenting the coast for several years. Both were English and ostensibly were friends. One, a Captain P.B., went to Gambia to trade and the other, a Captain C.P., went to Sherbro. Captain C.P., as was his custom, landed his goods and built a crude house to store them on shore. Then the storehouse burned, apparently by accident, and besides the goods, Captain C.P. lost the ship's papers and other valuable documents. He then set sail for Gambia where, Owen wrote, "he expected that his old frind Captain P.B. would help him . . . to make up his loss. Upon his arival he was receved with all marks of respect by his old frind. They drank and eat together and parted for the first night. In the morning Captain P.B. returned his vissit and in his company were seven or eight soldiers from the fort in order to saze [seize] Captain C.P., his ship and slaves by reason he had no papers on board. The poor man made all the deffence he could, but all to no porpose. He was sazed and is now trading among us here in a long boat, reflecting on that unnatureall villan who sacrafised his honour, friendship and all for the sake of ill got riches.

"You'll hardly meet with such an action of villany in these natives towards one another," Owen said. Captain C.P. wrote home of his misfortune and the House of Commons "has taken it into consideration to persequit Captain P.B. at law as soon as his arival."

January 1758. "Shiping is still growing scarscer, so that is the opinion of several that the whites will be obliged to go home if the war continues any considerable time. As for myself, I live in the station of a hermit and make myself contented with my pressent circumstances since I find it impossable to go off without a dail [deal] of danger and risque. Yet it's a deal of comfort to me that I can sit down in my own cabin, after all my sufferings and hardships and injoy fruts of a quiet retirement, which is a serenety of mind that a man can seldom attain to when he mixes with the busey part of mankind. I look upon the rest of the world as a scene of trouble and vanity. Europe, that ought to be the seet of all happyness that this life can afford, is now involv'd in bloodey wars and all other calamiteys atending it . . . Here I sit down and reflect upon both without any danger from either, excep the want of goods. Not but that I would suffer a great dail to do my country service in any quality so ever, but fortune has disposed of me otherwise and I must be contented with my lot without complaining."

January 10, 1758. "Capt. Engledue, upon his comeing up the river, refus'd the king his custum, which has bred a great pilaver between the king and all the whites, so that it's dangerous to pass or repass in the river. It has cost Mr. Tucker four or five bars and it is not finished yet."

Even the native kings were not safe from treachery. Tucker's brother, Peter, sought twice to kill him, and the King of Sheffra was poisoned by someone who dosed his pot of wine.

Later in March 1758, Owen confides his Irish past to his journal. His father had inherited a good estate from his grandfather and another large sum by his wife, Owen's mother, but through dissipation and with the help of a "pirticular law sute, sunk him two low to be able to provide for his children and his maner of life lost him the affections of his frinds and relations."

The relatives, Owen added, showed Owen and his remaining family resentment and ill will and when he resolved to leave when he was grown, "they aplauded my resolution in the highest manner and wished me a good voyage, but never once contributed to my circumstances by a giveing hand or shewed the least grain of pitey in my distresses . . . Ever since I have endavouer'd with the utmost aplycation to live independent of those wretches . . ."

He wrote that he intended to stay in Africa to "enlarge my fortune by honest mains [means], in a country where even its beastly inhabatants shews me more respect than those hardharted relations in the place of my birth."

October 1758. "I am now in a verry uncertain way, all my people has left me sick at home and four slaves in the house and I am not able to go anywhere to sell them. I have been in this condition ever since 20 Sepmr and see no sighns of relief, every one striving who shall to thief or steal most from me."

November 1758. Owen reports that he is recovering from his illness and "praparing for action again and exercise."

February 1759. "Lately we have the malloncoly news of Captain Potter's being cut off by the slaves at Mano and the ship drove ashoar. The captain, second mate and docter are all killed in a barbarous manner by the slaves. The slaves are all taken by the natives again and sould to other vessells, so that they have nothing mended their condition by their enterprize."

February 12, 1759. "Mr. Tucker's sons has arrived from Cape Mount, with several articles belonging to Captain Potter's vessel that hove on shoar."

And this was Owen's last entry in his journal. He died on March 26, 1759. The journal ends with this doleful postscript by his brother, Blayney.

"This fatal month makes the final period of the author's life . . . who left me to struggle with the world a little longer, disconsolate and alone amidst Negroes. No man can be ignorant of my affliction in the said circumstances, tho' in want of nothing, I mean the necessarys of life. My chief trust is in the Almighty, Who of His great mercy has given me a tranquillity of mind which is above what this world can give, and which alone sustains me amid the tempestuous waves of my severe affliction. He teaches me to look at every Christian as my brother and supply the place of the deceas'd which is some comfort to me, altho' it is but an imperfect imitation of his fraternall affection."

3

A SAILOR'S LIFE

THE GUINEA SLAVE SHIPS were fondly regarded by British admirals as a "nursery" for their seamen. In time of need, almost constant during the eighteenth century, sailors were readily impressed from the slave ships into the men-of-war. These seamen composed a vital commodity making up an important bulwark of defense for England.

But the belief that the English slave ships were the navy's basic training fleet was exploded as myth by Thomas Clarkson, an indefatigable abolitionist who spent years collecting facts and figures on the slave trade.*

According to Clarkson's findings, the losses of seamen aboard the Guinea ships were incredibly high. His figures showed that 21.5 percent of the English seamen aboard slave ships died on the voyages; this compared to the Privy Council's estimate in 1789 that 12.5 percent of the slaves transported in English vessels died en route. Adding those seamen who deserted or were discharged, on one pretext or another by captains who then collected the defaulted wages, Clarkson maintained that *less than half* of

* Thomas Clarkson, *History of the Rise, Progress and Accomplishment of the Abolition of the African Slave Trade, by the British Parliament.* London, 1808.

those seamen who sailed aboard Guinea-bound ships from England ever returned home again.

Clarkson laid his raw statistics before Parliamentary investigators and the public. From 1784 to 1790, 12,263 seamen sailed
from England aboard three hundred and fifty Guinea ships.
Only 5,760 returned home, many so diseased and emaciated that
they were fit only to spend their remaining days begging on the
wharves. Clarkson said 2,643 died in passage and the remainder
deserted or were discharged in Africa or the New World. Few of
the latter ever reached England again. Deserters in Africa were
brutally punished if caught, and they could expect little help
from the natives who willingly turned them in to collect rewards
or sold them into slavery.

Clarkson said that of every nine hundred and ten sailors in
each of the various commercial shipping routes followed by English vessels, thirty-seven would die on the long voyage to India
via the Cape of Good Hope, twenty-one in direct trade to the West
Indies, nine on trade vessels to Greenland, and two hundred on
the slave ships.

But Clarkson was not considered an impartial observer and it
remained for Sir George Young, a British naval commander, to
shock the nation awake to the tremendous drain in manpower
the slave trade represented. Sir George made a series of inspec-
tion trips to English outposts in Africa in the 1780's. In his report to Parliament investigators, he said the slave trade was "not
a nursery, but a grave for seamen."*

His statement, the official acknowledgement of the navy that
the horrors of the trade so loudly proclaimed by the abolitionists
did truly exist, was used as a major ax by the latter to hack at the
opposition.

* House of Commons, *Debate on the Motion for the Abolition of the Slave
Trade*. London, 1792.

Conditions aboard the ships grew so bad that in the latter part of the eighteenth century, few seamen readily signed aboard a Guineaman. African slave ships often laid in dock for months until a crew of thirty to forty men could be signed aboard. Those who did were forced aboard to relieve themselves of debts, to escape prison or were simply shanghaied at the last moment. Treatment was generally good and discipline relaxed until the ships were well out to sea. Then the luckless seamen found themselves in a hell where rations were suddenly shortened and punishment meted out for the slightest infraction. There were few violations that brought anything less than a flogging. The cat, an instrument of correction, was the common denominator for all Guinea seamen.

Guinea seamen were the most hard-bitten sailors in the world and a sailor's life until recent decades was at best one of the most dangerous occupations open to man. The seaman worked long hours, and frequently slept on deck because the holds were packed with trade goods or slaves. He had to be an aerial acrobat to work the shrouds in a gale-tossed sea day and night and still stay alive. Rations generally amounted to a pound of beef, a pound of bread, a half-pint of flour, peas or oatmeal.

When compared to English ships, conditions aboard American slaving vessels were said to be slightly better for the seamen. Most of the sailors were from New England where the captains and crews were from the same classless, democratic society. The loss of a seaman's life through the ill-tempered cruelty of a captain or mate could bring retribution by the victim's relatives or the courts when the ship returned home.

But slave captains, with few exceptions, succumbed to the temptation of open brutality. They were lords and masters aboard ship and in a slave ship discipline was paramount. The tinderbox situation with so many hostile slaves aboard could flame into disastrous mutiny at the slightest laxity. Some com-

manders reverted to brutes, disciplining their men excessively
— others, as James Stanfield describes, became monsters, per-
verted by licentiousness and the naked thrill of torture.

The following passages are drawn from first-person accounts
by Dr. Alexander Falconbridge, a witness to the torment and
degradation of seamen on the ships he sailed on, and by Stanfield,
who experienced them as a sailor. The first is by Falconbridge:*

"In one of these [voyages] I was witness to the following instance of cruel usage. Most of the sailors were treated with brutal
severity; but one in particular, a man advanced in years, experienced it in an uncommon degree. Having made some complaint
relative to his allowance of water, and this being construed into
an insult, one of the officers seized him, and with the blows he
bestowed upon him, beat out several of his teeth. Not content
with this, while the poor old man was yet bleeding, one of the
iron pump-bolts was fixed in his mouth, and kept there by a piece
of rope tied round his head. Being unable to spit out the blood
which flowed from the wound, the man was almost choked, and
obliged to swallow it. He was then tied to the rail of the quarter-
deck, having declared, upon being gagged, that he would jump
overboard and drown himself. About two hours after he was
taken from the quarter-deck rail, and fastened to the grating
companion of the steerage, under the half deck, where he remained all night with a centinel placed over him.

"A young man on board one of the ships was frequently beaten
in a very severe manner, for very trifling faults. This was done
sometimes with what is termed a cat (an instrument of correction which consists of a handle or stem, made of rope three
inches and a half in circumference, and about eighteen inches
long, at one [end] of which are fastened nine branches, or
tails, composed of log line, with three or more knots upon each

* Alexander Falconbridge, *An Account of the Slave Trade on the Coast of Africa.*
London, 1788.

[5 1]

branch) and sometimes he was beaten with a bamboo. Being one day cruelly beaten with the latter, the poor lad, unable to endure the severe usage, leaped out of one of the gun ports on the larboard side of the cabin, into the river. He, however, providentially escaped being devoured by the sharks, and was taken up by a canoe belonging to one of the black traders then lying alongside the vessel. As soon as he was brought on board, he was dragged to the quarter-deck, and his head forced into a tub of water, which had been left there for the negro women to wash their hands in. In this situation he was kept until he was nearly suffocated; the person who held him, exclaiming, with the malignity of a demon, 'If you want drowning, I will drown you myself.' Upon my inquiring of the young man, if he knew the danger to which he had exposed himself by jumping overboard, he replied 'that he expected to be devoured by the sharks, but he preferred even that, to being treated daily with so much cruelty.'

"Another seaman having been in some degree negligent, had a long chain fixed round his neck, at the end of which was fastened a log of wood. In this situation he performed his duty (from which he was not in the least spared) for several weeks, till at length he was nearly exhausted by fatigue; and after his release from the log, he was frequently beaten for trivial faults. Once, in particular, when an accident happened, through the carelessness of another seaman, he was tied up, although the fault was not in the least imputable to him, along with the other person, and they were both flogged till their backs were raw. Pepper was then mixed in a bucket, with salt water, and with this the harrowed parts of the backs of the unoffending seamen were washed, as an addition to his torture.

"The same seaman having on another time accidentally broken a plate, a fish-gig was thrown at him with great violence. The fish-gig is an instrument used for striking fish, and consists of several strong barbed points fixed on a pole, about six feet long, loaded at the end with lead. The man escaped the threatening danger, by stooping his head, and the missile struck in the barricado. Knives and forks were at other times thrown at him; and a large Newfoundland dog was frequently set at him, which thus encouraged, would not only tear his clothes, but wound him. At length, after several severe floggings, and other ill treatment, the poor fellow appeared to be totally insensible to beating and careless of the event.

"I must add here, that whenever any of the crew were beaten, the Newfoundland dog, just mentioned, from the encouragement he met with, would generally leap upon them, tear their clothes, and bite them. He was particularly inveterate against one of the seamen, who, from being often knocked down, and severely beaten, appeared quite stupid and incapable of doing his duty. In this state, he was taken on board another ship and returned to England.

"In one of my voyages, a seaman came on board the ship I belonged to, while on the coast, as a passenger to the West Indies. He was just recovered from a fever and notwithstanding this he was very unmercifully beaten during the passage, which, together with the feeble state he was in at the time, rendered him nearly incapable of walking, and it was but by stealth that any medical assistance could be given to him.

"A young man was likewise beaten and kicked almost daily, for trifling, and even imaginary faults. The poor youth happening to have a very bad toe, through a hurt, he was placed as a sentry over the sick slaves, a station which required much walking. This in addition to the pain it occasioned, increased a fever he already had. Soon after he was compelled although so ill, to sit on the gratings, and being there overcome with illness and fatigue, he chanced to fall asleep, which being observed from the quarter-deck, he was soon awakened and with many oaths upbraided for neglect of duty. He was then kicked from the gratings, and so cruelly beaten, that it was with great difficulty he crawled to one of the officers who was more humane, and complaining of the cruel treatment he had just received, petitioned for a little barley-water (which was kept for the sick slaves) to quench the intolerable thirst he experienced.

"Another seaman was knocked down several times a day, for faults of no deep dye. It being observed at one time, that the hen coops had not been removed by the sailors who were then washing the decks, nor washed under, which it was his duty to see done, one of the officers immediately knocked him down, then seized and dragged him to the stern of the vessel, where he threw him violently against the deck. By this treatment, various parts of his body was much bruised, his face swelled, and he had a bad eye for a fortnight. He was afterwards severely beaten for a trifling fault and kicked till he fell down. When he got on shore in the West Indies, he carried his shirt, stained with the blood which had flowed from his wounds, to one of the magistrates of the island, and applied to him for redress; but the ship being consigned to one of them, all the redress he could procure was his discharge.

"Many other instances of similar severity might be produced; but the foregoing will suffice to give some idea of the treatment seamen are liable to, and generally experience, in this employ; the consequence of which usually is desertion or death.

"Of the former, I will give one instance. While a ship I belonged to lay at Bonny, early one morning near a dozen of the crew deserted in one of the longboats. They were driven to this desperate measure, as one of them afterwards informed me, by the cruel treatment they had experienced on board. Two of them, in particular, had been severely beaten and flogged the preceding day. One of these having neglected to see that the arms of the ship were kept fit for use, was tied up to the mizen shrouds, and after being stripped, very severely flogged on the back; his trowsers were then pulled down, and the flogging was repeated. The other seaman, who was esteemed a careful, cleanly, sober fellow, had been punished little less severely, though it did not appear that he had been guilty at that time of any fault.

"It is customary for most of the captains of the slave ships to go on shore every evening to do business with the black traders. Upon these occasions many of them get intoxicated and when they return on board, give proofs of their inebriation by beating and ill using some or other of the crew. This was the present case; the seaman here spoken of, was beaten, without any reason being assigned, with a knotted bamboo, for a considerable time; by which he was very much bruised, and being before in an ill state of health, suffered considerably.

"Irritated by the ill usuage which all of them, in their turn, had experienced, they resolved to attempt an escape, and effected it early in the morning. The person on the watch discovered that the net-work on the main deck had been cut, and that one of the longboats was gone; and upon further examination it was found that near a dozen of the seamen were missing. A few hours after, the captain went in the cutter in pursuit of the deserters, but without success.

"On my return to England, I received from one of them the following account of their adventures during this undertaking. When they left the vessel, they proposed going to Old Calabar, being determined to perish rather than return to the ship. All the provisions they took with them was a bag containing about half a hundred weight of bread, half a small cheese, and a cask of water about 38 gallons. They made a small sail of a hammock, and erected one of the boat's oars for a mast. Thus slenderly provided, they dropped down the river of Bonny and kept along the coast; but mistaking one river for another, they were seized by the natives, who stripped them and marched them across the country for a considerable distance, to the place to which they themselves intended going. During the march, several were taken ill, and some of them died. Those who survived were sold to an English ship which lay there. Every one of these deserters, except three, died on the coast, or during their passage to the West Indies; and one of the remaining three died soon after his arrival there. So that only two out of the whole number lived to arrive in England, and those in a very infirm state of health.

"While I am upon the subject of the desertions among the sailors, I must add, that the captains in this trade generally take out with them tobacco and slops, which they sell at an exorbitant price to the sailors. And in case of their desertion or decease, they have it in their power to charge to the seamen's accounts whatever quantity they please without contradiction. This proves an additional reason for cruel usage. In case of desertion, the sailors forfeit their wages, by which the expenses of the voyage are lessened, and consequently the merchants reap benefits from it."

James Stanfield was a seaman aboard slave vessels for a number of years and at the request of Thomas Clarkson wrote a series of letters describing a sailor's life in the Guinea trade.*

"It has been asserted that the slave trade is a desirable employ and a nursery for our seamen.

"Were this the case, sailors would be found as willing to offer themselves to this as to any other traffic. But the direct contrary is the fact. Nothing is more difficult than to procure a sufficient number of hands for a Guinea voyage.

"To collect a crew for this purpose, there are public houses, under the influence and in the pay of merchants. Every allurement and artifice is held out to entice them into these infamous dens. Festivity and music lay hold of the deluded senses, prostitution throws in a fascinating spell with too much success, and intoxication generally gives the business its fatal period.

"In these houses, every temptation to run to debt is most studi-

* James F. Stanfield, *The Guinea Voyage and Letters.* London, 1807.

ously offered; this, with an unthinking sailor, is easily brought about. And when once that wheel is set in motion, it is soon accelerated to the wretched point which was aimed at. When the debt is sufficient for the purpose, a Guinea ship is offered, sometimes through the medium of the inexorable hostess, and frequently by one of those numerous agents on that business, who under the mask of pity or sudden friendship, win the attention and confidence of the unsuspecting victim. If this be refused, he is thrown into prison, which fixes him their own; for from that place, other vessels will scarcely engage him. Ships in every other employ finding seamen willing enough to offer their services, and the captains of these have a natural objection to what they call jail-birds.

"These houses are kept in continual operation. But, at the immediate time of an outfit, every exertion and contrivance is used. Merchants, clerks, captains and others prowl about without intermission. They lay hold of every sailor they meet, and without ceremony, hurry him into some scene of intoxication. I have been dragged into houses three times, in the course of one street myself. Nay, I have known many seamen who fancied themselves cunning enough to evade these practices, go with the crimps to some of their houses, boasting that they would cheat the merchant out of a night's merriment, and firmly resolved to oppose every artifice that could be offered, yet have they, in their state of drunkenness signed articles with the very men whose purposes they were aware of, and have been plunged into a situation, of which they had known the horrors.

"In Liverpool — and I understand that the same practice prevails at Bristol — when they have signed articles, they get a note for their advance money, not payable till they are out at sea, and till a list of the crew is brought back by the pilot. Now to negotiate this bill, which is to pay their debts, and to furnish themselves with a few clothes, and a little modicum of liquor, they are obliged to make a will, and power of attorney, in favour of their rapacious landlady. The third mate of the vessel I sailed in — poor Russel, — and myself were obliged to give into this practice. Without any idea of debt, and far from any of those hired dens I have mentioned, but rather reputably lodged in what they called a coffee-house, we found it absolutely necessary, in order to live with any degree of ease and comfort, to make wills in favour of our landlady. It was expected as a thing of course, and was impossible to avoid moderately. Her brewer, a man of credit, was the witness and leader of the business, and seemed to consider it as an essential consequence of the voyage. It is true, we cancelled them soon by new ones, but this may serve to show the prevalency of the practice, and may help to exhibit to the public, the disinterested characters of that numerous body of men, women and children who have with such cogent arguments signed the Liverpool petition against the abolition of the slave trade — those whip-cord spinners, those chain-forgers, those heirs and legatees, deriving inheritance from the cruelty, murder and injustice of a Guinea voyage.

[The petition which Stanfield mentions was signed by hundreds of Liverpool residents, declaring to Parliament that the end of the slave trade would bring about their economic ruin.]

". . . Till the vessel gets clear of the channel — till there is no probability that contrary winds or inclemency of weather will drive her back into an English port, the usage of the seamen is moderate, and their allowance of provisions sufficient; in short, the conduct of the captain and officers appears like that which is the continual practice in every other employ. But as soon as they are fairly out at sea, and there is no moral possibility of desertion, or application for justice, then the scene is shifted. Their ration of provisions is shortened to the very verge of famine; their allowance of water lessened to the extreme of existence;

nothing but incessant labour, a burning climate, unremitting cruelty, and every species of oppression is before them.

"This is no exaggerated language, nor is it the picture of one particular case. Every one I have ever spoken with, that was qualified to answer on the subject . . . has declared that the usage was alike, with but a few exceptions . . .

"We were fortunate in a leaky vessel, and bad weather. The apprehension that we should be obliged to bear away for Lisbon, kept back our misery for awhile. Flogging did not commence till about the latitude 28 degrees. It was talked of long before, but was with-held by the above-mentioned consideration. It no sooner made its appearance, but it spread like contagion. Wantonness, misconception, and ignorance, inflicted it without an appearance of remorse, and without fear of being answerable for the abuse of authority. This barbarous charge to the officers I myself heard given. 'You are now in a Guinea ship. No seaman, though you speak harshly, must dare to give you a saucy answer. That is out of the question, but if they look to displease you, knock them down.'

"The cruel direction was soon put into practice by one of the mates on the cooper, a most harmless, hard-working worthy creature. The mate knocked him down for some light answer he gave him, for the poor fellow had an innocent aim at being humorous. On his making his way to appeal to the captain, he was knocked down again. Crawling on the deck, his face covered with blood, he still persisted to make his way to the cabin, but was struck to the deck a third and fourth time, when some of the sailors rushed between, and hurried him away.

"Scarcely an hour passed in any day without floggings; sometimes three were tied together. The slightest imputation of error brought on the bitter punishment; and sometimes the smarting application of pickle was superadded.

"I do not now exactly remember the allowance of bread. At first I know it was five pounds per week, served out every Sunday (the only circumstance that distinguished the Sabbath through the whole voyage) but it was soon lessened. This I very well remember, that many of the people had their whole week's proportion eaten up by Tuesday morning, and the daily weight of beef was so small, that though there was no water to allay the thirst it occasioned, we never dared to steep it for fear of wasting the quantity.

"During the first part of the passage, our allowance of water was three pints per day. For the last month it was reduced to one quart, wine measure. A quart of water in the torrid zone! . . . In the calms, which are prevalent in this latitude, we were in the boat, towing, from morning till night. Happy used I to think myself, though almost fainting with fatigue, if a little sweat dropped from my forehead, that I might catch it in my mouth to moisten my parched tongue. The licking the dew off the hencoops in the morning had been long a delicious secret; but my monopoly was at last found out, and my little refreshment laid open to numbers. Many of the men could not refrain, but in a mind of temporary distraction, from drinking up their whole allowance the moment they received it, and remained for the next four and twenty hours in a state of raging thirst not to be described. The doctor declared that this want of water, in such a climate and living entirely on salt provisions, must lead to the most fatal consequences.

"During this scarcity with the men, the captain, besides plenty of beer and wine, had a large tea-kettle of water every morning, and another every evening, added to his allowance. I know there was no want in the cabin, for the third mate, who was my friend, frequently gave me a little out of his own portion.

"The scarcity of water is a common case. It is owing to the vessel's being stowed so full of goods, for the trade, that room for

necessaries is made but a secondary consideration. The occasion
of this conduct appears to me to be principally this: A certain
number of slaves are to be carried to the West Indies. But before
that number can be landed there, the owners are well aware how
many are likely to be marked on the dead list, for the purchase
of which there must be goods sent out, as well as for the probable
number that speculation has fixed to come to market. For this
reason every corner and cranny is crammed with articles of
traffic. To this consideration is bent every exertion of labour and
ingenuity, and the health and lives of the seamen, as of no value,
have but little weight in the estimation . . .

"The vessel is so crowded with goods that the sailors have no
room to sling their hammocks and bedding. Before they leave
the cold latitudes they lie up and down, on chests and cables, but
when they come nearer the influence of the potent sun, they
sleep upon deck, exposed to all the malignity of the heavy and
unwholesome dews . . .

"I am fully convinced that if a commerce was carried on to the
coast of Africa of any other kind than that of slaving, and the
captains treated their people with as much humanity as they
treated in other employs, not one of the causes of the great mortality I have been witness to could exist.

"Among the many causes of destruction, which originate from
the trade, and not from the climate, the bulk-heads between the
decks, excluding a salutary circulation of air, have been insisted
upon as producing these effects. But there is another which has
not claimed such notice, and which yet is a terrible assistant to
African mortality. This is the fabricating of an house over the
vessel for the security of slaves, while on the coast.

"This enclosure helps the stagnation of air, and is, in that point
of view, dreadful. But it is more fatal in the fact of its preparation. I know nothing more destructive than the business of cutting wood and bamboe, for the purpose of erecting and thatch-

ing this structure. The process is generally by the riverside. The faces and bodies of the poor seamen are exposed to the fervour of a burning sun, for a covering would be insupportable. They are immersed up to the waist in mud and slime; pestered by snakes, worms and venomous reptiles; tormented by muskitoes and a thousand assailing insects. Their feet slip from under them at every stroke, and their relentless officers do not allow a moment's intermission from the painful task. This employment, the cruelty of the officers, and the inconceivably shocking task of scraping the contagious blood and filth at every opportunity from the places where the slaves lie are, in my opinion, the three greatest (though by no means the sole) causes of destruction of seamen, which this country experiences by the prosecution of the trade in slaves . . .

"It is unaccountable, but it is certainly true, that the moment a Guinea captain comes in sight of this shore, the Demon cruelty seems to fix his residence within him. Soon after we arrived, there came on board us a master of a vessel, who was commissioned joint factor with our captain. All that I could conceive of barbarity fell short of the stories I heard of this man. His whole delight was in giving pain.

"While our captain was placing buoys and other directions on the dangerous bar of the river for the purpose of crossing it, he used to order the men to be flogged without an imputation of the smallest crime. The steward, for serving out some red wine to the sick men, by the doctor's direction, was flogged in such a manner as not to be able to let his shirt touch his mangled back; and after his punishment, making an attempt to explain the matter, he was ordered to the shrowds again, and the same number of lashes was repeated.

"It was his common practice to call his cabin boy to him, and without the slightest provocation, to tear his face, ears and neck, in the most brutal manner. I have seen him thrust his fingers into his mouth and force them against the inside of his cheek till the wound appeared on the outside of the same. He had pulled his ears so much that they became of a monstrous size. The hind part of them was torn from the head. They had a continual soreness and running, and were not well near a twelve month after his infernal tormentor's death, when he [the cabin boy] deserted from us in the West Indies. I heard many and uncommon stories of the barbarity of this monster to his own crew, but had an opportunity to see but little of him, for he lived but eleven days after he came on board us. He killed himself with our wine and beer, of which he had not tasted any for a long time before our arrival there.

"At the commencement of our trade, I went up to the factory, where I continued about eight months. In the course of this time most of the crew fell the sacrifices of this horrid traffick and its inseparable cruelties. One evening only was I on board during this period. . . . The vessel was like a slaughter house. Blood, filth, misery and disease. The chief mate lay dying, calling out for that comfort and assistance he had so often denied to others. He was glad to lay hold of me to bring him a little refreshment — no one else would take the smallest notices of his cries. The doctor was in the same condition, and making the same complaint. The second mate was lying on his back on the medicine-chest, his head hanging down over one end of it, his hair sweeping the deck and clotted with the filth that was collected there, and in this unnoticed situation he died soon after I came on board.

"On the poop the appearance was still more shocking — the remainder of the ship's crew stretched in the last stage of their sickness, without comfort, without refreshment, without attendance. There they lay, straining their weak voices with the most lamentable cries for a little water, and not a soul to afford them the smallest relief. And while all this horror and disease were preying on the lives of the poor seamen, the business of purchasing, messing the slaves, and every circumstance relative to the trade was transacting with as little interruption, and as much unconcern as if no such people had ever been on board.

"To provide against this mortality, and to convey the purchase to the West Indies . . . a fine large ship, and a fresh crew were sent out to us. The new captain, and a few to make trade, were left behind in the factory. About five of the old crew, all that were now left, and in the last stage of illness were brought off with us. In this fresh ship, and with this fresh crew, we left the coast and entered on what is called the middle passage. This horrid portion of the voyage was but one continued scene of barbarity, unremitting labour, mortality and disease. Flogging, as in the outward passage, was a principal amusement in this.

"The captain was so feeble that he could not move, but was obliged to be carried up and down. Yet his illness, so far from abating his tyranny, seemed rather to increase it. When in this situation, he has often asked the persons who carried him whether they could judge of the torment he was in? And being answered, no, he had laid hold of their faces and darting his nails into their cheeks with all his strength; on the person's crying out with the pain, he would then add, with the malignity of a demon, 'There, that is to give you a taste of what I feel.'

"To the post of [his] bed he would order those to be tied that were to be flogged, so that their faces almost met his, and there he lay, enjoying their agonized screams, while their flesh was lacerated without mercy. This was a frequent and favourite mode of punishment . . .

"The cook one day burned some meat in the roasting. He was called to the cabin on that account, and beaten most violently with the spit. He begged and cried for mercy, but without effect, until the strength of his persecutor was exhausted. He crawled somewhere — but never did duty afterwards. He died in a day or two.

"The poor creatures, as our numbers thinned, were obliged to work when on the very verge of death. The certainty that they could not live a day longer, did not procure them a grain of mercy. The boatswain, who had left the coast a healthy hearty man, had been seized with the flux. He was in the last stage of it, but no remission from work was allowed him.

"He grew so bad at last that the mucus, blood and whole strings of intestines came from him without intermission. Yet, even in this situation — when he could not stand — he was forced to the wheel, to steer a large vessel, an arduous duty, that in all likelihood would have required two men had we had people enough for the purpose. He was placed upon one of the mess-tubs, as not being able to stand, so that he might not dirty the deck. He remained at this painful duty as long as he could move his hands — he died on the same night. The body was, as usual, thrown overboard, without any covering but the shirt. It grew calm during the night and continued to be so for a good part of the next day — in the morning his corpse was discovered floating alongside and kept close to us for some hours — it was a horrid spectacle and seemed to give us the idea of the body of a victim calling out to heaven for vengeance on our barbarity.

"As the crew fell off, an accumulated weight of labour pressed upon the few survivors and towards the end of the middle passage all idea of keeping the slaves in chains were given up; for there was not enough strength left among the white men, to pull a single rope with effect. The slaves (at least a great number of them) were therefore freed from their irons and they pulled and hauled as they were directed by the inefficient sailors. We were fortunate in having favourable weather; a smart gale of wind, such as with an able crew would not have created us more trouble than reefing our sails, must have inevitably sent us to destruction . . .

"In this state of weakness . . . but little attention could be paid to those whose approach to the last stage of their misery renders helpless and in want of aid. I remember that a man who was ill had one night crawled out of his hammock. He was so weak that he could not get back, but laid himself down on the gratings. There was no one to assist him — in the morning, when I came on deck — I shudder at the bare recollection he was still alive, but covered with blood — the hogs had picked his toes to the bone and his body was otherwise mangled by them in a manner too shocking to relate . . .

"Flogging, that favourite exercise, was in continual use with the poor Negroes as well as the seamen. So incessant was the practice, that it is impossible to discriminate the particular occasions or circumstances. One or two, however, I may mention.

"Just before we left the coast, and when the rooms were so crowded that the slaves were packed together to a degree of pain, there came a boat-load of slaves alongside in the night, after all those on board had been put below. The new comers were also put down, to shift for themselves, and of course much noise ensued. In the women's room, this was sadly increased by one of the strangers being so unfortunate as to be thrown down a certain tub. In the morning she was tied up to the captain's bed, with her face close to his, and a person was ordered to flog her. The idea of the sex operating on the unwilling executioner, she did not receive her punishment with all the severity that was expected. The executioner was himself tied up, and for the leniency he had shown, received a violent lashing. The woman was then flogged till her back was full of holes. I remember that in healing them they were so thick that I was forced to cut two or three of them into one to apply the dressings."

Stanfield was aware that the gruesome stories he had related in his letters to the young abolitionist Clarkson could draw doubt because of their horror, so he added:

"No pen, no abilities can give more than a very faint resemblance of the horrid situation. One real view — one minute, absolutely spent in the slave rooms on the middle passage, would do more for the cause of humanity, than the pen of a Robertson, or the whole collective eloquence of the British senate."

4

A GUINEA VOYAGE

SLAVE SHIP VOYAGES were long, sometimes lasting several years, and they often became grim trials of illness, despair and death for captains, crew and cargo alike. There is little need to fictionalize the account of the hardships and hazards faced by the mariners of the Atlantic slave trade. Captain Thomas Phillips, master of the *Hannibal* of London, leaves a stark picture of life aboard his ship on a slaving voyage to Africa in 1693 and 1694. The matter-of-fact entries perhaps make the horror of his experiences even more vivid.*

He begins the journal shortly after his return home from a voyage to the Mediterranean, a trip which was interrupted when he was captured by three French men-of-war off the coast of Ireland. He was imprisoned briefly in France before obtaining his release. Back in England, he was approached by Sir Jeffrey Jeffreys and other investors and retained to purchase and equip the *Hannibal*, a ship of four hundred and fifty tons and thirty-six guns. At that, Phillips and his backers were licensed by the Royal African Company to sail in its service on a slaving voyage to Africa. At that time the Royal African Company was the only

* Thomas Phillips, "Journal." *A Collection of Voyages and Travels*, Vol. VI. Edited by Awnsham and John Churchill. London, 1746.

concern which had sanction of the crown to carry on slaving commerce. On September 5, 1693, Phillips left London for Gravesend where the ship was anchored, arriving aboard at 11 P.M. The next day he paid his crew their river pay and one month's advance pay, according to the agreement they had signed when they joined the ship. On September 12, the *Hannibal* left the Thames estuary and traveled down the coast in a convoy with at least four other ships for protection against French warships.

Not long after the *Hannibal* had cleared the English Channel, a woman was discovered masquerading as one of the Royal African Company's soldiers bound for a Guinea Coast trading station. Phillips dealt with her gently.

"I order'd her a private lodging apart from the men and gave the taylor some ordinary stuffs to make her woman's cloaths, in recompence for which she prov'd very useful in washing my linen and doing what else she could, till we deliver'd her with the rest at Cape Coast Castle, on the coast of what is now Ghana. She was about twenty years old and a likely black girl."

A violent storm scattered the convoy and damaged the *Hannibal*. His officers were all for returning to England for repairs but Phillips declared his resolve to proceed with the journey "though I should be forced to go with a jury-mast . . ."

A few days later the *Hannibal*, traveling alone, was overtaken by a French frigate and attacked. "The fight lasted six hours, from four till ten o'clock, being all that while within pistol shot, little wind, and small water and firing as fast as both sides could load our guns. We often gave them *huzza's* during the engagement and they would answer with *Vive le roys*."

The frigate finally veered away, but left the *Hannibal* with five men dead, thirty-two wounded and the ship badly riddled with shot. The crew spent the next three days repairing the damage, then headed for Santiago, in the Cape Verde Islands, to refit.

After weeks there, the *Hannibal* sailed on and reached Cape
Mesurado on the African coast on December 23. There Phillips
found the *Hannibal*'s consort, the *East-India Merchant*. The two
ships had left England together and had been parted by the
storm.

From Mesurado, the *Hannibal* and *East-India Merchant*
traveled down the coast together in search of trade. The *East-
India Merchant*'s skipper, Captain Shurley, fell ill not long after
the two ships arrived on the coast. Captain Phillips's log continues as they began looking for slaves to purchase.

January 13. "We came to anchor in nine fathom [of] water
off the, river of Sestos yesterday about four in the evening. . . .
This morning I went ashore with some goods to trade and Capt.
Shurley sent his with his purser, being so ill that he could not go
himself. . . . About eight miles up the river is the town where King
Peter their monarch lives, but I could not spare time to go and
visit him, and in truth had no great inclination to venture so far
in a boat, having been inform'd that the Negroes here are very
treacherous and bloody, as some of our European traders have
found to their cost."

January 14. "Finding no trade to encourage our stay at Sestos,
we got up our stream-anchor this morning and set sail with a
small gale at W."

January 15. "At ten we were off the river Sino . . . from when
came several canoos aboard us with pepper, or, as they call it,
malagetta . . . I bought 1000 weight of it to give to our Negroes in
their messes to keep them from a flux and dry belly-ache, which
they are very incident to . . ."

January 17. "Yesterday my poor brother grew very ill and de-
lirious, and notwithstanding all the endeavours used by my own
and Captain Shurley's doctor for his recovery, about three in the
evening he took his leave of this troublesome world, and left me
full of affliction for the loss of him. He had been sick of malignant

fever about eight days and many of my men lay ill of the same distemper."

January 18. "We got under sail, when the coffin being ready, the deceas'd was nailed up therein; and our pinnace being hoisted out, he was lower'd into her. Myself, my doctor and purser went in her to bury him, the colours of our own ship and the *East-India Merchant* being lower'd half-mast down, our trumpets and drums sounding and beating, as is customary upon such melancholy occasions. We row'd the corpse about ¼ of a mile from the ship to seaward; and the prayers of the church being read, I helped to commit his body to the deep, which was the last office that lay in my power to do for my dear brother. Then the *Hannibal* fired sixteen guns at ½ minute distance of time, which was the number of years he had lived in this uncertain world, and the *East-India Merchant* fired ten guns. . . ."

January 21. "At six we weigh'd anchor and stood along to the east. About ten, two canoos came aboard us from *Caba-la-ho* and were follow'd by several others with stores of good teeth [of elephants], which invited us to come anchor. But ere the Negroes in the canoos would come aboard, they required the captain of the ship should come down the outside of the ship and drop three drops of the sea water into his eye as a pledge of friendship and of safety for them to come aboard . . . I have no where upon the coast met with Negroes so shy as here, which makes me fancy they have had tricks played upon by such blades as Long Ben, alias Avery, who have seiz'd them and carried them away."

The two ships continued down the coast, trading along the way. On February 20, they reached Succandy where the Royal African Company had a station. "We found the factor, Mr. Johnson, in his bed raving mad, cursing and swearing most wretchedly at us, not in the least knowing Capt. Shurley, tho' he had a long former acquaintance with him. I pity'd from my soul this poor man, who had plunged himself into this condition thro' resentment of an affront put upon him by one Vanbukeline, the merchant of the Mine-Castle."

Johnson's youthful assistant told the visiting captains the story behind the trader's wretchedness. The English factor, or trader, had taken a fancy several years earlier to an eleven-year-old mulatto girl. He brought her and her mother to his station, which was more a fort because of the times, to live until the girl became "of age fit for matrimonial functions." Johnson's intentions, quite questionable anywhere else, seemed normal on the African Coast. In the meantime, Vanbukeline, a neighboring Dutch trader, saw the girl at Johnson's station and also desired her. He bribed the girl's mother and had the two spirited to his own fort where, according to Johnson's assistant, he "soon cracked that nut which Mr. Johnson had been so long preparing for his own tooth."

The theft of his young maiden and some other old differences between him and the Dutchman "did so disturb" Johnson "and vex him that it threw him into distempers and quite turned his brain," said Phillips. Phillips said also that he later visited Vanbukeline's station and saw the young prize there, bearing the title of Madame Vanbukeline. "I have been informed that since my being there, that the adjacent Negroes, instigated by Vanbukeline and the Dutch general [at the station], had in the night surprized and seized the fort, cut Johnson to pieces and plundered all the goods and merchandize."

March 27. "In the afternoon we came to an anchor at Cabo Corce [Cape Coast Castle, the principal fort of the Royal African Company] and saluted our castle with 15 guns, which they returned . . . We landed out of the *Hannibal* at this place thirty soldiers for the company, in as good health as we received them aboard in England; but in two months time that we lay here to complete our business, they were near half dead, and scarce enough of the survivors able to carry their fellows to the grave . . .

"At Cabo Corce we took in part of the Indian corn ordered us for the provision of our Negroes to Barbadoes, the allowance being a chest which contains about four bushels for every Negro . . ."

April 25. "This morning we took our leave of the castle, paying our respects with fifteen guns, which they return'd, it being too late to salute them last night . . ."

The *Hannibal* and her consort traveled the short distance to Animabo, where the Royal African Company operated two small stations. Mr. Searle, the factor at one, and Mr. Cooper, the factor at the other, entertained the two ship captains. "Mr. Cooper, who is a very ingenious young gentleman, gave us a cordial reception, having the company of his wife (as he call'd her) to dine with us, as we had of Mrs. Searle's at Animabo, both being mulattoes. This is a pleasant way of marrying, for they [the factors] can turn them off and take others at pleasure; which make them very careful to humour their husbands, in washing their linen, cleaning their chambers, etc., and the charge of keeping them is little or nothing."

Captain Phillips said the inhabitants of Animabo were "accounted very bold and stout fellows, but the most desperate treacherous villains, and the greatest cheats upon the whole coast, for the gold here is accounted the worst, and most mix'd with brass, of any in Guinea . . ."

May 4. "This morning at eight we made sail, and eleven came to an anchor at Winiba in nine fathom good ground. Having moor'd ship after dinner, went ashore . . . We fill'd some water and cut good store of fire-wood by the queen's permission. This queen is about fifty years old, as black as jet, but very corpulent.

"We went with Mr. Buckerige [the local factor] to pay our respects to her under a great tree where she sat. She received us very kindly and made her attendants dance after their manner before us. She was very free of her kisses of Mr. Buckerige, whom she seemed much to esteem, and truly he deserved it from [those who] knew him, being an extraordinary good-humoured and ingenious gentleman, and understood this country and language very well. We presented her with an anchor of brandy each, and some hands of tobacco, which she received with abundance of thanks and satisfaction, and so bid her good night. She was so extremely civil before we parted to offer each of us a bed-fellow of her young maids of honour while we continued there, but we modestly declined her majesty's proffer, and that night lay ashore with Mr. Buckerige. . . ."

May 9. "Our business being compleated at Winiba, we went aboard and got our ships under sail for Acra . . . Capt. Shurley has been long sick of a flux and fever and is now very ill, and I troubled with violent convulsions in my head, that I can get no sleep without opiates, and so giddy that I cannot walk without assistance. . . ."

May 12. (At Acra [Accra, on what is now the coast of Ghana]). "Captain Thomas Shurley, commander of the *East-India Merchant*, my consort, departed this life here, having been long sick of a fever and flux. He was handsomely buried at Acra Castle, a la Soldado, his own ship firing guns at half a minute distance, during the time the corpse was rowed ashore . . . After he was buried, according to the service of the church of England, his own ship fired 20 guns, the *Hannibal*, 26, Acra fort, 20, and the Dutch and Black's fort, 16 each."

May 20. "This morning about nine o'clock we arrived at Whidaw [Ouidah, in what is now Togo], being about sixty leagues from Acra to the east, and let go our anchor in eight fathom water, about two miles off shore. . . . This day we got our canoos and all things else ready, in order to go ashore tomorrow to purchase our slaves."

The first leg of their voyage completed, the following portion of his journal provides one of the best descriptions available of the trading methods then in practice on the coast. Captain

Phillips sets out deliberately to describe the problems he faced, the difficulties of dealing with native businessmen and the treatment of the Negroes he had purchased. On May 21, Captain Phillips, accompanied by Mr. Clay, his former first mate and now captain of the *East-India Merchant*, and the doctors and pursers of both ships and about a dozen of their seamen for a guard, moved ashore to live for the following nine weeks. They would remain until they could buy thirteen hundred Negro slaves — seven hundred for the *Hannibal* and six hundred and fifty for the *East-India Merchant*.

Phillips describes Whidaw as "being the pleasantest country I have seen in Guiney, consisting of champaigns [fields and flat, open country] and small descending hills, beautified with always green shady groves of lime, wild orange, and other trees, and irrigated with divers broad fresh rivers, which yield plenty of good fish; towards the sea-shore it is very marshy and has divers large swamps.

"Our factory at Whidaw lies about three miles from the seaside where we were carried in hamocks . . . It stands low near the marshes, which renders it a very unhealthy place to live in. The white men the African Company send there seldom returning to tell their tale. 'Tis compass'd round with a mud wall about six feet high, and on the southside is the gate; within is a large yard, a mud thatch'd house, where the factor lives, with the white men; also a storehouse, a trunk for slaves, and a place where they bury the dead white men, call'd, very improperly, the hog-yard. There is also a good forge and some other small houses. To the east are small flankers of mud, with a few popguns and harquebusses, which serve more to terrify the poor ignorant Negroes than to do any execution. While we were here the factor made a wide deep ditch, round the factory, and had my carpenters to make a draw-bridge over it, which has render'd it now pretty secure; for before it was enterable every rainy time, the walls being washed down, and when the rains were over, built up again.

"And here I must observe that the rain season begins about the middle of May and ends the beginning of August, in which space it was my misfortune to be there, which created sickness among my Negroes aboard, it being noted for the most malignant season by the blacks themselves, who, while the rains last, will hardly be prevail'd upon to stir out of their huts. Myself and the poor men found it so by dear experience, the rains that fall down then being more like fountains than drops, and as hot as if warmed over a fire.

"The factory is about 200 yards in circumference, and a most wretched place to live in, by reason of the swamps adjacent, whence proceed noisome stinks, and vast swarms of little flies, call'd musketoes, which are so intolerably troublesome, that if one does not take opium, laudanum, or some other soporifick, 'tis impossible to get any sleep in the night . . .

"I had not lain down above an hour in the factor's bed, but I was so vex'd and tormented by those little malicious animals that I was forced to get up again and dress myself, put gloves on my hands, and tie a handkerchief over my face till day-light, which notwithstanding those troublesome devils would sting thro', and the place so stung would much inflam'd and rise into a knob, much provoking the exercise of a man's nails; and had King James the first been there some time, he would have been convinc'd that scratching where it itches was not the greatest pleasure in the world, as 'tis said was his opinion . . .

"After we had procured a parcel of slaves and sent them down to the sea-side to be carry'd off, it sometimes proved bad weather, and so great a sea, that the canoos could not come ashore to fetch them, so that they returned to the factory, where they were secured and provided for till good weather presented, and then were near to embrace the opportunity, we sometimes shipping off a hundred of both sexes at a time.

"We had our cook ashore and eat as well as we could, provisions being plenty and cheap, but we soon lost our stomachs by sickness, most of men having fevers, and myself such convulsions and aches in my head, that I could hardly stand or go to the trunk without assistance, and there often fainted with the horrid stink of the Negroes, it being an old house where all the slaves are kept together and evacuate nature where they lie, so that no jakes can stink worse; there being forced to sit three or four hours at a time, quite ruin'd my health, but there was no help . . .

"When we were at the trunk, the king's slaves, if he had any, were the first offer'd to sale . . . I observ'd they were generally the worst slaves in the trunk, and we paid more for them than any others, which we could not remedy, it being one of his majesty's prerogatives. Then the cappasheirs* each brought out his slaves according to his degree and quality . . . and our surgeon examined them well . . . to see that they were sound wind and limb, making them jump, stretch out their arms ·swiftly, looking in their mouths to judge of their age; for the cappasheirs are so cunning that they shave them all close before we see them, so that . . . we can see no grey hairs in their heads or beards. Then having liquor'd them well and sleek with palm oil, 'tis no easy matter to know an old one from a middle-aged one, but by the teeths decay.

"But our greatest care of all is to buy none that are pox'd, lest they should infect the rest aboard; for tho' we separate the men and women aboard by partitions and bulk-heads, to prevent

* Cappasheirs were the king's principal attendants, who occupied positions similar to dukes. Phillips said a new king was elected from among the cappasheirs when the old king died.

quarrels and wranglings among them, yet do what we can they will come together, and that distemper which they call the yaws is very common here, and discovers itself by almost the same symptoms as the *Lues Venerea* or clap does with us; therefore our surgeon is forc'd to examine the privities of both men and women with the nicest scrutiny, which is a great slavery, but what can't be omitted.

"When we had selected from the rest such as we liked, we agreed in what goods to pay for them, the prices being already stated before the king, how much of each sort of merchandize we were to give for a man, woman, and child, which gave us much ease and saved abundance of disputes and wranglings, and gave the owner a note, signifying our agreement of the sorts of goods; upon delivery of which the next day he receiv'd them. Then we mark'd the slaves we had bought in the breast, or shoulder, with a hot iron, having the letter of the ship's name on it, the place being before anointed with a little palm oil, which caused but little pain, the mark being usually well in four or five days, appearing very plain and white after.

"When we had purchased to the number of 50 or 60, we would send them aboard, there being a cappasheir, intitled the captain of the slaves, whose care it was to secure them to the waterside and see them all off. If in carrying to the marine any were lost, he was bound to make them good to us, the captain of the trunk being oblig'd to do the like, if any run away while under his care, for after we buy them we give him charge of them till the captain of slaves comes to carry them away. There are two officers appointed by the king for this purpose, to each of which every ship pays the value of a slave in what goods they like best for their trouble, when they have done trading; and indeed they discharg'd their duty to us very faithfully, we not having lost one slave thro' their neglect in thirteen hundred we bought here.

"There is likewise a captain of the sand, who is appointed to take care of the merchandise we have come ashore to trade with, that the Negroes do not plunder them, we being often forced to leave goods a whole night on the sea shore, for want of porters to bring them up; notwithstanding his care and authority, we often came by the loss and could have no redress.

"When our slaves were come to the sea-side, our canoos were ready to carry them off to the longboat, if the sea permitted and she convey'd them aboard ship, where the men were all put in irons, two and two shackled together, to prevent their mutiny, or swimming ashore.

"The Negroes are so wilful and loth to leave their own country, that they have often leap'd out of the canoos, boat and ship, into the sea, and kept under water till they were drowned, to avoid being taken up and saved by our boats, which pursued them; they having a more dreadful apprehension of Barbadoes than we can have of hell, tho' in reality they live much better there than in their own country, but home is home, etc.

"We have likewise seen divers of them eaten by the sharks, of which a prodigious number kept about the ships in this place, and I have been told will follow her hence to Barbadoes, for the dead Negroes that are thrown overboard in the passage. I am certain in our voyage there we did not want the sight of some every day, but that they were the same I can't affirm. We had about 12 Negroes did wilfully drown themselves, and others starved themselves to death; for 'tis their belief that when they die they return home to their own country and friends again."

Phillips discusses the problems of trade, noting that cowries, or the shells which served as money in that section of the coast, were the best goods used to purchase slaves. Then came brass basins, which were cut into bracelets by the natives. After that the captain could use coral, iron, cloth such as chintz, for trade, but Phillips warns that a slave ship commander had to be wary of making a true report of his trade goods to the king and his minions. "If they can discover that you have a good store of cowries and brass aboard, then no other goods will serve their turn, till they have got as much as you have; and after [that] for the rest of the goods they will be indifferent and make you come to their own terms, or else lie a long time for your slaves so that those you have on board are dying while you are buying others ashore . . ."

Phillips advises that if there is more than one ship in the place, the captains should agree on what they will announce as their cargoes to prevent the above situation. But he admits this seldom happened. ". . . For where there are divers ships, and of separate interests, about buying the same commodity, they commonly undermine, betray and outbid one the other and the Guiney commanders' words and promises are the least to be depended upon of any I know who use the sea, for they would deceive their fathers in their trade if they could."

The ship was anchored a mile and a half off shore, in heavy swells and a strong surf ran constantly. "We venture drowning every time we go ashore and come off, the canoos frequently over-setting, but the canoomen are such excellent divers and swimmers that they preserve the lives of those they have any kindness for, but such as they have any displeasure to they will let shift for themselves. Therefore 'tis very prudent for all commanders to be kind and obliging to them, their lives lying in their hands, which they can make them lose at pleasure, and impute all to accident, and they could not help it; and there are no amends to be had . . .

"When our slaves are aboard we shackle the men two and two, while we lie in port, and in sight of their own country, for 'tis then they attempt to make their escape and mutiny. To prevent this we always keep sentinels upon the hatchways, and have a chest of small arms, ready loaden and prim'd, constantly lying at hand upon the quarter-deck, together with some granada shells, and two of our quarter-deck guns pointing on the deck thence, and two more out of the steerage, the door of which is always kept shut and well barr'd.

"They are fed twice a day, at 10 in the morning and 4 in the evening, which is the time they are aptest to mutiny, being all upon deck; therefore all that time, those of our men who are not employ'd in distributing their victuals to them, and settling them, stand to their arms; and some with lighted matches at the great guns that yawn upon them, loaded with partridge, till they have done and gone down to their kennels between decks. Their chief diet is call'd dabbadabb, being Indian corn ground as small as oat-meal in iron mills, which we carry for that purpose; and after mix'd with water and boil'd well in a large copper furnace, till 'tis as thick as a pudding. About a peckful of which in vessels, call'd crews, is allow'd to 10 men, with a little salt, malagetta and palm oil, to relish.

"They are divided into messes of ten each, for the easier and better order in serving them. Three days a week they have horse-beans boil'd for their dinner and supper, great quantities of which the African Company sends aboard for that purpose. These beans the Negroes extremely love and desire, beating their breast, eating them and crying *'Pram, Pram'* which is *'Very good.'* They are indeed the best diet for them, having a binding quality, and consequently good to prevent the flux, which is the inveterate distemper that most affects them, and ruins our voyages by their mortality.

"The men are all fed upon the main deck and forecastle, that we may have them all under command of our arms from the quarter-deck, in case of disturbances. The women eat upon the quarter-deck with us and the boys and girls upon the poop. After they are once divided into messes, and appointed their places, they will readily run there in good order of themselves afterwards. When they have eaten their victuals clean up (which we

[8 3]

force them to for to thrive the better), they are order'd down between decks, and every one as he passes has a pint of water to drink after his meat [meal], which is serv'd them by the cooper out of large tub, fill'd beforehand ready for them.

"When they have occasion to ease nature, they are permitted by the centinels to come up and go to [a] conveniency which is provided for that purpose on each side of the ship, each of which will contain a dozen of them at once, and [they] have broad ladders to ascend them with the greater ease.

"When we come to sea we let them all out of irons, they never attempting then to rebel, considering that should they kill or master us, they could not tell how to manage the ship, or must trust us, who would carry them where we please. Therefore the only danger is while we are in sight of their own country, which they are loath to part with; but once out of sight out of mind. I never heard that they mutiny'd in any ships of consequence, that had a good number of men, and the least care. But in small ships where they had but few men, and those negligent or drunk, then they surprized and butcher'd them, cut the cables, and let the vessel drive ashore and everyone shift for himself.

"However, we have some 30 or 40 Gold Coast Negroes, which we buy and are procur'd us there by our factors, to make guardians and overseers of the Whidaw Negroes, and sleep among them to keep them from quarrelling, and in order, as well as to give us notice, if they can discover any caballing or plotting among them, which trust they will discharge with great diligence. They also take care to make the Negroes scrape the decks where they lodge every morning very clean, to eschew any distempers that may engender from filth and nastiness. When we constitute a guardian, we give him a cat of nine tails as a badge of his office, which he is not a little proud of and will exercise with great authority.

"We often at sea, in the evenings, would let the slaves come

up into the sun to air themselves, and make them jump and
dance for an hour or two to our bag-pipes, harp and fiddle, by
which exercise to preserve them in health; but notwithstanding
all our endeavour, 'twas my hard fortune to have great sickness
and mortality among them."

With this note of the misery his ship was to undergo, Phillips
narrates the middle passage of the *Hannibal*.

"Having bought my complement of 700 slaves, 480 men and
220 women, and finish'd all my business at Whidaw, I took my
leave of the old king and his cappasheirs, and parted, with many
affectionate expressions on both sides, being forced to promise
him that I would return again the next year, with several things
he desired me to bring from England . . . I set sail the 27th of
July in the morning, accompany'd with the *East-India Merchant,*
who had bought 650 slaves, for the Island of St. Thomas . . . from
which we took our departure on August 25th and set sail for
Barbadoes.

"We spent in our passage from St. Thomas to Barbadoes two
months eleven days, from the 25th of August to the 4th of November following: in which time there happened such sickness
and mortality among my poor men and Negroes. Of the first we
buried 14, and of the last 320, which was a great detriment to
our voyage, the Royal African Company losing ten pounds by
every slave that died, and the owners of the ship ten pounds ten
shillings, being the freight agreed on to be paid by the charter-
party for every Negro delivered alive ashore to the African Company's agents at Barbadoes. . . . The loss in all amounted to near
6500 pounds sterling.

"The distemper which my men as well as the blacks mostly
died of was the white flux, which was so violent and inveterate
that no medicine would in the least check it, so that when any
of our men were seized with it, we esteemed him a dead man, as
he generally proved. I cannot imagine what should cause it in

them so suddenly, they being free from it till about a week after we left the island of St. Thomas. Next to the malignity of the climate, I can attribute it to nothing else but the unpurg'd black sugar and raw unwholesome rum they bought there, of which they drank in punch to great excess, and which it was not in my power to hinder, having chastised several of them and flung over-board what rum and sugar I could find, and was forced to clap one Lord, our trumpeter, in irons for his being the promoter of their unseasonable carousing bouts, and going in one of his drunken fits with his knife to kill the boatswain in his bed, and committing other enormities. But tho' he remained upon the poop day and night in irons for two months, without any shelter than the canopy of heavens, he was never troubled with any sickness, but made good the proverb, *That naught's never in danger*, or *That he who is born to be hang'd*, etc . . .

"The Negroes are so incident to the small-pox that few ships that carry them escape without it, and sometimes it makes vast havock and destruction among them. But tho' we had 100 at a time sick of it, and that it went thro' the ship, yet we lost not above a dozen by it. All the assistance we gave the diseased was only as much water as they desir'd to drink, and some palm-oil to anoint their sores, and they would generally recover without any other helps but what kind nature gave them.

"One thing is very surprizing in this distemper among the Blacks, that tho' it immediately infects those of their own colour, yet it will never seize a white man; for I had several white men and boys aboard that had never had that distemper, and were constantly among the Blacks that were sick of it, yet none of them in the least catch'd it, tho' it be the very same malady in its effects, as well as symptoms, among the Blacks as among us in England, beginning with the pain in the head, back, shivering, vomiting, fever, etc.

"But what the smallpox spar'd, the flux swept off, to our great regret, after all our pains and care to give them their messes in due order and season, keeping their lodgings as clean and sweet as possible, and enduring so much misery and stench so long among a parcel of creatures nastier than swine, and after all our expectations to be defeated by their mortality."

After that incredibly bitter statement, Phillips adds: "No gold-finders can endure so much noisome slavery as they do who carry Negroes; for those have some respite and satisfaction, but we endure twice the misery; and yet by their mortality our voyages are ruin'd, and we pine and fret ourselves to death, and take so much pains to so little purpose."

The *Hannibal* reached Barbados in the first part of November 1694, where Phillips delivered three hundred and seventy-two Negroes still alive to the company's agents, who in turn sold them for nineteen pounds per head. The *Hannibal* loaded aboard seven hundred hogsheads of sugar, some cotton and ginger, but had to wait until April of 1695 to accompany an armed convoy back to England. Finally, on April 2, 1695, with thirty other merchant ships and naval vessels under the protection of the man-of-war *Tiger*, they set sail. Phillips was about two weeks at sea when he was seized again by the old illness from the Guinea Coast.

"The vertigo was much allay'd soon, but the convulsions continued so severe upon that I was forced for most part to keep to my bed." A month later, he began to lose the hearing of his left ear, having already lost the hearing of his right ear on the Guinea Coast. The ship's surgeon had died of the plague in Barbados and Phillips's condition daily grew worse.

"When I came to London, thro' the kindness and goodwill of my friends and acquaintances, who were sorry to see me return in that condition, I was advised to a great many applauded physicians, who all pretended they would cure my deafness. I went under the care of several of them, who were the most celebrated in that famous city, by whose orders I was tormented by the apothecaries, with doses of nasty physick every day, for four or five months time, and butcher'd by the surgeons with blisters, issues, setons, etc., and spent about 100 guineas among them, without receiving a farthing benefit. Wherefore I did conceive it more prudence to bear my deafness as contentedly as I could, then any longer to undergo so much misery and charge to no purpose.

"Accordingly I shook hands with the doctors and being rendered unfit for my employment by my deafness, I settled my affairs in London, took my leave of it, and came down to Wales, among my relations in Brecknock, my native town, there to spend the rest of my life as easily as I can under my hard misfortune."

5

DEATH IN THE HOLD

As SEEN IN THE PREVIOUS CHAPTER, disease often took a large toll of slaves and crews in the middle passage. Malaria, smallpox, dysentery, scurvy, ophthalmia, plus countless African jungle maladies for which there were no names, or cures, could turn an entire ship into a pestilential trap for everyone aboard.

Medical knowledge in those years was limited, but the disease that broke, little matter what its name, was freely abetted by the conditions aboard ship in doing its very worst. There were two schools of thought as to how to transport slaves, and these had a direct effect on how much havoc an epidemic inflicted. Some captains favored giving each slave plenty of room, thus giving each and all a better chance for health en route. But the other school said pack them together; don't worry about the loss from disease because those who survived would more than make up the cost of the dead.

Ruthless ship captains would throw over the side the first slave or two to show any evidence of sickness, thus hoping to prevent its spread. Others threw overboard sick slaves who would certainly bring low prices in the West Indies. Insurance rates were high, but they covered the loss of jettisoned cargo. It remained to the final court decision in the case of the slave ship *Zong* to halt this practice.

The *Zong*, a British slave ship captained by Luke Collingwood, had sailed from Africa in September 1781, with four hundred and forty slaves on board. As they neared the Caribbean islands, Collingwood called together a few officers to discuss disposition of more than a hundred sick slaves. According to a witness, the master, Collingwood, said that "if the slaves died a natural death, it would be the loss of the owners of the ship; but if they were thrown overboard alive into the sea, it would be the loss of the underwriters." The witness then said that Collingwood added, "It would not be so cruel to throw the poor sick wretches into the sea, as to suffer them to linger out a few days under the disorders with which they were afflicted . . ."*

In the next few days, Collingwood selected one hundred and thirty-three sick slaves, "all or most of whom were sick or weak, and not likely to live, and ordered the crew by turns to throw them into the sea; which most inhuman order was cruelly complied with." Later, the owners sought to collect from the underwriters back in Liverpool and the latter, learning of the circumstances, balked and refused to pay. The owners won the suit in a lower court, but the underwriters carried it to a higher court and secured a reversal of the decision.

Packing the maximum number of slaves in a vessel was an unscrupulous art which captains prided themselves upon. There was little or no regard for the slaves' comfort. They were packed in rows like so many spoons, each man lying on his side with no more than ten to sixteen inches between them. Thus they would remain for weeks during the voyage across the ocean, unable to get topside for fresh air if the weather were bad or the captain feared the risk were too great.

* Elizabeth Donnan, *Documents Illustrative of the History of the Slave Trade to America.* Vol. II. Washington, 1931.

Ophthalmia was a scourge not uncommon aboard slave ships but about which little was known in the way of a cure. It was a common disease in some sections of the African coast and slave captains carefully examined their purchases to eliminate any infected with it. The voyage of the *Le Rodeur*, a French vessel, is one of the most famous stories in French medical history and though its authenticity is somewhat dubious, it is offered as a narrative that became a legend a century ago. For gripping melodrama, it is one of the most intriguing stories of the slave trade.

The account is supposedly by J. B. Romaigne, a twelve-year-old lad who wrote his mother of his voyage across the Atlantic. He was the son of a West Indian planter and was being sent there as a passenger on the *Le Rodeur* under the special watch of the captain. The slaver sailed from Le Havre for the Calabar river and anchored at Bonny in March 1819. During the next three weeks one hundred and sixty Negroes were purchased and loaded. The ship then sailed for the French West Indies.

"It is now just a week since we sailed; but indeed, it is not my fault that I have not sooner sat down to write. The first two days I was sick, and the other five were so stormy that I could not sit at the table without holding. Even now we are rolling like a great porpoise yet I can sit very well and keep the pen steady. Since I am to send you what I do without copying it over again at the end of the voyage, I shall take what pains I can; but I hope, my dear mother, you will consider that my fingers are grown hard and tarry with hauling all day on the ropes, the Captain being determined, as he says, to make me a sailor. The Captain is very fond of me and is very good-tempered; he drinks a great deal of brandy; he is a fine, handsome man and I am sure I shall like him very much.

"I enquired of the Captain today, how long it would be before we should get to Guadaloupe; and he told me we had a great distance to go before we should steer that way at all. He asked how I should like to have a little black slave and I said very well; that I was to have plenty of them at Guadaloupe. He asked me what I could do with them. 'Feed them,' I said. 'That is right,' said the Captain; 'it will make them strong. But you will make them work won't you?' added he. 'Yes, to be sure,' said I. 'Then I can tell you must flog them as well as feed them.' 'I will,' said I, 'it is what I intend, but I must not hurt them very much.' 'Of course not maim them,' returned he, 'for then they would not work; but if you do not make them feel to the marrow, you might as well throw them into the sea."

"Since we have been at this place, Bonny Town in the Bonny River, on the coast of Africa, I have become more accustomed to the howling of these negroes. At first, it alarmed me, I could not sleep. The Captain says that if they behave well they will be much better off at Guadaloupe; and I am sure, I wish the ignorant creatures would come quietly and have it over. Today, one of the blacks whom they were forcing into the hold, suddenly knocked down a sailor and attempted to leap overboard. He was caught, however, by the leg by another of the crew, and the sailor, rising up in a passion, hamstrung him with a cutlass. The Captain, seeing this, knocked the butcher flat on the deck with a handspike. 'I will teach you to keep your temper,' said he, with an oath. 'He was the best slave in the lot.' I ran to the main chains and looked over; for they had dropped the black into [the] sea when they saw that he was useless. He continued to swim, even after he had sunk under water, for I saw the red track extending shoreward; but by and by, it stopped, widened and faded and I saw it no more."

"We are now fairly at sea again, and I am sure my dear mother, I am heartily glad of it. The Captain is in the best temper in the world; he walks the deck, rubbing his hands and humming

a tune. He says he has six dozen slaves on board, men, women
and children, and all in prime marketable condition. I have not
seen them, however, since we set sail. Their cries are so terrible
that I do not like to go down and look into the hold. At first, I
could not close my eyes; the sound froze my very blood; and, one
night, jumping up in horror, I ran to the Captain's state-room.
The lamp shone upon his face; it was as calm as marble. He
slept profoundly, and I did not like to disturb him."

"Today, word was brought to the Captain, while we were at
breakfast, that two of the slaves were dead, suffocated, as was
supposed, by the closeness of the hold; and he immediately ordered the rest should be brought up, gang by gang, to the forecastle, to give them air. I ran up on deck to see them. They did
not appear to me to be very unwell; but these blacks, who are not
distinguished one from another by dress, are so much alike one
can hardly tell.

"However, they had no sooner reached the ship's side, than
first one, then another, then a third sprang up on the gunwale,
and darted into the sea, before the astonished sailors could tell
what they were about. Many more made the attempt, but without success; they were all knocked flat to the deck, and the crew
kept watch over them with handspikes and cutlasses till the Captain's pleasure should be known with regard to the revolt.

"The negroes, in the meantime, who had got off, continued
dancing about the waves, yelling with all their might, what
seemed to me a song of triumph and they were soon joined by
several of their companions still on deck. Our ship speedily left
the ignorant creatures behind; their voices came fainter and
fainter upon the wind; the black head, first of one, then another,
disappeared, and then the sea was without a spot; and the air
without a sound.

"When the Captain came up on deck, having finished his

breakfast, and was told of the revolt, his face grew pale. 'We must make an example or our labour will be lost,' he said. He then ordered the whole of the slaves in the ship to be tied together in gangs and put on the forecastle, and having selected six, who were known to have joined in the chorus of the revolters and might thus be considered as the ringleaders, he caused three of them to be shot, and the other three hanged before the eyes of their comrades."

"Last night I could not sleep; cold sweats broke over my body. I thought the six negroes were passing to and fro through the cabin, and looking in at the door of the Captain's stateroom. The Captain, I could hear, was sound asleep, and this made me more afraid. At last I began to pray so loud, that I awoke him, and he asked me what was the matter. 'I am saying my prayers,' said I. 'That is a good boy,' replied he, and, in an instant he was sound asleep as before.

"The negroes, ever since the revolt, were confined closely to the lower hold and this brought on a disease called ophthalmia, which produces blindness. The sailors, who sling down the provisions from the upper hold, report that the disease is spreading frightfully and today, at dinner, the Captain and the surgeon held a conference on the subject. The surgeon declared that from all he could learn the cases were already so numerous as to be beyond his management; but the Captain insisted that every slave cured was worth his value and that it was better to lose a part than all. The disease, it seems, although generally fatal to the negro, is not always so. The patient is at first blind; but some escape, eventually, with the loss of one eye or a mere dimness of vision. The result of the conversation was, that the infected slaves were to be transferred to the upper hold and attended by the surgeon the same as if they were white men."

"All the slaves and some of the crew are blind. The Captain, the surgeon and the mate are blind. There is hardly enough men left out of our twenty-two, to work the ship. The Captain preserves what order he can and the surgeon still attempts to do his duty, but our situation is frightful.

"All the crew are now blind but one man. The rest work under his orders like unconscious machines; the Captain standing by with a thick rope, which he sometimes applies, when led to any recreant by the man who can see. My own eyes begin to be affected; in a little while, I shall see nothing but death. I asked the Captain if he would not allow the blacks to come up on deck. He said it was of no use; that the crew, who were always on deck, were as blind as they; that if brought up, they would only drown themselves, whereas, if they remained where they were, there would, in all probability, be at least a portion of them salable, if we ever had the good fortune to reach Guadaloupe.

"We rolled along on our dreadful pain, with no other steersman than fate; for the single individual of the crew who was our last hope, now shares our calamity.

"You cannot comprehend our situation. It will not do to figure yourself tossing on the black and midnight deep, with not a star to cheer you, and not a hand to help; for even then you could see; you could see the glitter of the waters and the white crest of the wave and half see, half conjecture, the form of the objects around you. In the midst of all, you would at least possess an absolute conviction that, in a few hours more, a new sun would rise out of the ocean, a new morning dawn upon the world.

"Our night was not like that of the sea, the darkness of which is mingled with light like the first memory of day and relieved by the certainty of approaching morning. We were blind, stone blind, drifting like a wreck upon the ocean and rolling like a cloud before the wind. The Captain was stone blind, yet had hopes of recovering his sight, while most of the others were in despair. A guard was continually placed with drawn swords at the storeroom to prevent the men getting at the spirit-casks and dying in the frenzy of intoxication. Some were cursing and swearing from morning till night, some singing abominable songs; some kissing the crucifix and making vows to the blessed saints. A few lay all day long in their hammocks, apparently content to starve than look for food. For my part, I snatched at anything I could get to eat; cooking was unthought of. I thought myself fortunate when I was able to procure a cup of water to soften a biscuit which was as dry and hard as a stone."

"Mother, your son was blind for ten days, although now so well as to be able to write. I can tell you hardly anything of our history during that period. Each of us lived in a little dark world of his own, peopled by shadows and phantasms. We did not see the ship, nor the heavens, nor the sea, nor the faces of our comrades.

"Then there came a storm. No hand was upon the helm, not a reef upon the sails. On we flew like a phantom ship of old, that cared not for wind or weather, our masts straining and cracking; our sails bursting from their bonds, with a report like that of musketry; the furious sea one moment devouring us up, stem and stern, and the next casting us forth again, as if with loathing and disgust. Even so did the whale cast forth Jonah. The wind, at last, died away and we found ourselves rocking, without progressive motion, on the sullen deep. We at length heard a sound upon the waters, unlike that of the smooth swell which remained after the storm, and our hearts beat with a hope which was painful from its suddenness and intensity. We held our breath. The sound was continued; it was like the splashing of a heavy body in smooth water; and a simultaneous cry arose from every lip on deck and was echoed by the men in their hammocks below and by the slaves in the hold.

[97]

"Our cry was answered. We shouted again, our voices broken by sobs, and our burning eyes deluged with tears. Our shout was still answered; and for some minutes nothing was heard but an exchange of eager cries. The Captain was the first to recover his self-possession, and our voices sank into silence when we heard him speak to the approaching vessel with the usual challenge.

" 'Ship Ahoy! Ahoy! What ship?'

" 'The *Saint Leon* of Spain. Help us for God's sake.'

" 'We want help ourselves,' replied our Captain.

" 'We are dying of hunger and thirst. Send us on board some provisions and a few hands to work the ship and name your own terms.'

" 'We can give you food, but we are in want of hands. Come on board us and we will exchange provisions with you for men,' answered our Captain.

" 'Dollars! Dollars! We will pay you in money, a thousand fold, but we cannot send anyone. We have negroes on board; they have infected us with ophthalmia, and we are all stone-blind.'

"At the announcement of this horrible coincidence, there was a silence among us, for some moments, like that of death. It was broken by a fit of laughter, in which I joined myself; and, after a moment, before our awful merriment was over, we could hear by the sound of the curses which the Spaniards shouted at us that the *Saint Leon* had drifted away.

"This vessel, in all probability, foundered at sea, as we never learned of her ever reaching port."

"The man who preserved his sight the longest recovered the soonest. To his exertions alone, under the providence of God and the mercy of the blessed saints, is it owing that we are now within a few leagues of Guadaloupe, this twenty-second day of June 1819. I am myself almost well. The surgeon and eleven more are irrecoverably blind; the Captain has lost one eye; four others have met with the same calamity; and five are able to see, though dimly, with both. Among the slaves, thirty-nine are completely blind and the rest blind of one eye or their sight otherwise injured.

"This morning the Captain called all hands on deck, negroes and all. The shores of Guadaloupe were in sight. I thought he was going to return God thanks publicly for our miraculous escape.

" 'Are you quite certain,' said the mate, 'that the cargo is insured?'

" 'I am,' said the Captain. 'Every slave that is lost must be made good by the underwriters. Besides, would you have me turn my ship into a hospital for the support of blind negroes? They have cost us enough already. Do your duty.'

"The mate picked out thirty-nine negroes who were completely blind, and, with the assistance of the rest of the crew, tied a piece of ballast to the legs of each. The miserable wretches were then thrown into the sea."

6

ARRIVAL IN THE INDIES

IN ALL LIKELIHOOD, one of the islands in the Lesser Antilles was the luckless slave's first view of the New World on the western side of the Atlantic Ocean. Most slave ships traditionally made their first call there after the long crossing, usually for water and food before resuming the voyage to one of the slave markets on another island farther to the north and west, or on the mainland. But the largest markets were in the West Indies themselves. Agents who retailed the black flesh to plantations elsewhere gathered in the large island slave marts for their wares.

These islands represented the end, or nearly the end of the traumatic middle passage, of months aboard ship, crowded, jostled, thirsting and weakened by disease. The slave's chains hung heavier with each passing day, and the thought of relief from the dreadful rolling sea was revived by the sight of the green mountain isles. He was anxious to swap the ship for anything on land, no matter if he knew nothing of where he was or what his future held.

This desperation, of course, was not shared by anyone topside or those on shore who watched the approaching sails with the speculative interest in profits ahead. Bryan Edwards, a member of the Jamaica Assembly and a planter and slave owner, wrote a history of the West Indies in the eighteenth century. His attitude was probably typical of that of other slave owners:*

"Although there is something extremely shocking to the humane and cultivated mind in the idea of beholding a numerous body of our unfortunate fellow creatures in captivity and exile, exposed naked to publick view, and sold like a herd of cattle, yet I could never perceive that the Negroes themselves were oppressed with many of those painful sensations which a person unaccustomed to the scene would naturally attribute to such apparently wretchedness . . . They commonly express great eagerness to be sold, presenting themselves with cheerfulness and alacrity for selection and appearing mortified and disappointed when refused."

There was little need to understand the slave's emotions except in those circumstances which would affect his sale price. Some traders had no hesitancy in splitting up families whereas others felt they sold better as a group, since the separated Negroes pined and weakened themselves fretting over their loved ones.

The barbarous treatment of slaves in the West Indies plantations was notorious. On the West Indian sugar plantations the demand for fresh slaves was constant, if only to fill the ranks of those who were killed by the labor of getting in the crop. The slaves were regarded as unthinking beasts, but to say that their spirit had been completely subdued would be to ignore the numerous, bloody slave revolts in the history of the islands. These revolts were horrible swings of the pendulum and the memory of them would strike cold fear into white men for years afterwards.

There were attempts to correct the abuses, though their effec-

* Bryan Edwards, *The History, Civil and Commercial, of the British Colonies of the West Indies.* London, 1794.

tiveness was questionable. In 1792, the Consolidated Slave Act of Jamaica restricted punishments that could be imposed on slaves, and provided penalties for mutilating them. An incurable mutilation, for example, brought freedom to the injured slave and ten pounds a year for his upkeep. But it was no easy task to prove the charge against a white man, since the slave had no legal standing in court.

The following pages are devoted mainly to giving a picture of the arrival of two slave ships after the Atlantic voyage. The descriptions are by Dr. George Pinckard, a member of the Royal College of Physicians in Great Britain, who accompanied a British military expedition to the West Indies in 1795 as deputy inspector-general of the hospitals for the army.*

The period was the heyday of slave shipping and Dr. Pinckard wrote profuse and detailed letters home, filling them with descriptions of the islands, the people, the way of life, the climate, and just about every aspect of life that came within his purview.

Through his somewhat florid style, we see what Dr. Pinckard witnessed aboard an American and then a British slave ship which had just arrived in the West Indies. Dr. Pinckard innocently confesses that he saw nothing of the horror he had expected to view. This naive attitude is possibly explained later in his discussion of the health problems of transporting troops across the Atlantic as compared to slaves. He confides that he found the slaves, though far more crowded, to be healthier.

The following is Dr. Pinckard's account of his experiences while he was in Barbados, the easternmost island port in the Lesser Antilles:

"I have wished to visit the ships trading to Africa and to witness personally the manner of treating those poor beings of sable skins who are torn from their native land by the iron hand of commerce, to be transported to the home of slavery . . .

* Dr. George Pinckard, *Notes on the West Indies*. London, 1806.

"A slave ship belonging to North America and bound to Savanna in Georgia had arrived from the coast of Guinea just before we came into harbour and was lying very near to us with a cargo of Negroes on board.

"We considered ourselves fortunate in finding both the master and the mate of the slave ship disposed to show us every civility, and to indulge us in ready reply to the questions which our curiosity suggested.

"A little before they made Carlisle Bay they had been taken out of their ship and detained a whole night on board an English frigate while their papers were examined under the suspicion that the vessel and cargo were Dutch property, but the property being proved to be American, they were released and the ship is now taking in water, preparatory to pursuing her voyage down to the state of Georgia.

"The cargo consisted of a hundred and thirty slaves, of whom two-thirds were males and one-third females. The two sexes were kept separate by a partition, or bulk-head, built from side to side, across the ship, allotting the waist to the men, and to the women, the quarterdeck. A great majority of them were very young, being from ten to eighteen years of age. We were pleased to observe that an air of cheerfulness and contentment prevailed among them. In a few only we remarked despondency, and dejection of countenance. Both sexes were without apparel, having only a narrow band of blue cloth put around the waist, and brought to fasten before, so as to serve the office of a fig-leaf, worn by our first parents in the fruitful garden of Eden.

"As we walked through the different groups of them, they fixed their eyes upon us, with seeming curiosity, and some of the boys, like those of fairer skin, were inclined to be playful and exhibit youthful tricks. One or two of the females, unchecked by the reserve of education, occasionally glanced an expressive look or displayed a significant gesture. Many of them had marks upon

the skin which appeared to have been made by a cutting instrument. These, we learned, were distinctive of the nation to which
they belonged. Some had their teeth cut, or filed to sharp points,
giving them a very hideous and canine appearance. They looked
well fed and healthy, although some had an eruption, called the
cra-cra upon the skin.

"Their sleeping births were the naked boards. Divided into two
crowded parties, they reposed during the night upon the bare
planks below — the males on the main deck — the females upon
the deck of the aft cabin. In the daytime they were not allowed to
remain in the place where they had slept, but were kept mostly
upon the open deck, where they were made to exercise, and encouraged by the music of their loved banjar, to dancing and
cheerfulness.

"We saw them dance, and heard them sing. In dancing they
scarcely moved their feet, but threw about their arms and twisted
and writhed their bodies into a multitude of disgusting and in-
decent attitudes. Their song was a wild and savage yell, devoid of
all softness and harmony, and loudly chanted in harsh monotony.

"Their food is chiefly rice which they prepare by plain and
simple boiling. At the time of messing they squat around the
bowl in large bodies, upon their heels and haunches, like mon-
kies, each putting his paws into the platter to claw out the rice
with his fingers. We saw several of them employed in beating the
red husks off the rice, which was done by pounding the grain in
wooden mortars with wooden pestles sufficiently long to allow
them to stand upright while beating the mortars placed at their
feet. This appeared to be a labour of cheerfulness. They beat
the pestle in tune to the song and seemed happy; yet nothing of
industry marked their toil, for the pounding was performed by
indolently raising the pestle and then leaving it to fall from its
own weight.

"I am most happy to conclude my report of this visit by informing you that we discovered no marks of those horrors and cruelties said to be practiced on board the ships occupied in this sad traffic of human flesh, and which are represented so frightfully augmenting the manifold ills of slavery. Chains, stripes and severities did not seem to have been in the catalogue of means employed in conveying these poor Africans to their American masters."

It is sufficient to note here that many slave ship masters regularly began improving the treatment and food and relaxing discipline near port. The intent was obvious — to fatten the slaves and improve their demeanor to benefit their appearance in the marketplace.

"Our minds, necessarily, suffered in contemplating the degrading practices of civilized beings towards the less cultivated brethren of their species; but the eye was not shocked by the abuses of tyranny and inhumanity. The comfort and health of the slaves were promoted with every care. Being fond of washing in cold water, they were encouraged to free use of it; and their persons, as well as the whole of the ship, were kept remarkably clean. They were plentifully fed, and in the daytime were dispersed about the ship, so as to be prevented as much as possible from assembling together in close unwholesome crowds. Mirth and gaiety were promoted among them. They were roused to bodily exercise and care was used to divert their minds from dwelling upon their change of state and loss of home; and I may truly say, that a more general air of contentment reigned among them than could have been expected. While many were dancing and singing and playing together, others were giving their assistance in working the ship; and we even learned that several of them had made themselves mightly useful on the passage and were already becoming expert sailors.

"They all seemed to regard the master of the vessel more in affection than fear; and although strictly obedient, they did not appear to be at all under the influence of terror. Crowded in some degree, they necessarily must be, particularly in the place where they slept; but every attention was paid to prevent the injury which might derive from it; and to keep them in health."

(Compared with other accounts of the medical attention afforded slaves, particularly by Dr. Alexander Falconbridge, whose narrative is given in Chapters 3 and 7, the American ship was a luxury liner.)

"We went down below to see their place of repose, where the hard planks formed one common bed, and each individual employed his arms as his pillow. The men could not stand between the decks without stooping; and when they lay down, the boards were so closely spread, that it was scarcely possible to set a foot between their naked bodies. They were always taken upon deck early in the morning, and the sleeping birth was thoroughly cleansed and washed, but still it was highly offensive to European olfactories, and plainly indicated that were it not for the great attention paid to cleanliness and ventilation, disease must inevitably be generated.

"Their nakedness is, perhaps, their best security; for although they had neither bed-clothes, nor personal clothing, nor any kind of baggage, or furniture in the place, we perceived that all the cleaning and airing employed could not subdue the stench created by their sleeping together in such crowded heaps.

"The wool of their heads forms a thick cover for vermin, of which they have commonly a swarming abundance. Therefore, to prevent this, and to further the rules of cleanliness, all their heads had been shaved. But this, we were told, had deprived them of one great source of occupation and amusement, it being a singular pleasure to them to sit down in pairs for hours together, to enjoy the social feast of picking each other's heads, and afterwards twisting and plaiting the wool into a variety of forms.

"The pleasure we have experienced from finding these poor blacks in a state of apparent contentment, and with respect to the reported cruelty, enjoying a degree of comparative comfort, was succeeded by feelings of horror . . ."

The ship's officers, said Dr. Pinckard, then told the physician and his companions of a bloody insurrection on board just before leaving the African coast.

"Many of the Negroes had been detained on board for a considerable time while the cargo was being completed, lying during the period within sight of their native shore, from which and perhaps from their wives and families, they were about to be torn forever, had grown indignant even to desperation and rising upon the ship's company, murdered the master and mate and wounded several of the men. Nor was it over until after a severe and bloody contest they were overcome and the ringleaders were put to death as an example to deter others from again revolting. One of the sailors showed us three deep wounds which he had received on the face, the breast and the arm from the stroke of an axe, with which one of the blacks had just before struck off the captain's head.

"The next day, after our visit to the American slave ship, an opportunity offered of seeing one of our nation — a Liverpool Guineaman. It was a ship of much greater burden, fitted out expressly for the trade, with a sufficient number of hands and of guns to protect her against the enemy's privateers; and calculated for a cargo of five hundred slaves.

"We were taught to believe that we should find the Negroes much better accommodated in this, than in the American ship; but we could not observe that the superiority was either great, or striking. Although the vessel was larger, the number of slaves was more than proportionally greater. In other respects the accommodations were nearly equal. The Liverpool ship was kept remarkably clean; but the American was not less so; and between the decks, the American ship was commodious, being higher and having more room in proportion to the cargo, from which the slaves had the advantage of being less close and confined during the night.

"In the sleeping place of the English vessel we could not stand up without stooping almost double — in each the men and women were kept separate — in both their food was rice; and in both they slept naked upon naked planks, crowded together like sheep in a fold.

"The most striking difference that occurred to our observation was that the slaves of the Liverpool ship were of blacker and smoother skin than the others, and all of them free from that dirty eruption, the cra-cra. But upon our noticing this better appearance of one cargo than the other, the apparent superiority was instantly explained to us, by the observation that the Liverpool vessel had reached her destined port, and that her cargo had been made up for market by having their skins dressed over three or four times with a compound of gun-powder, lime-juice and oil — a preparation which not only destroys the cra-cra and gives the skin a smooth, black and polished appearance, but likewise renders it sleek and fine. And it was further remarked that the cargo of the American ship would be made to look as well before they reached the port where they were to be exposed for sale."

Having just crossed the ocean aboard a troopship, Dr. Pinckard compares the customary methods of transporting English soldiers with those used to carry slaves.

"Where from three hundred to five hundred men, in addition to the ship's company, have to make a passage in the same vessel, they cannot but be crowded. And if the weather should chance to be bad, it will be impossible to have the lower deck kept so clean, and well ventilated as is requisite. Hence from many of the soldiers becoming sick, from their taking food in their sleeping births, and crowding themselves with knapsacks, blankets and other baggage; and from multitudes breathing together, in so close and confined place, the air must very quickly be rendered unwholesome, and disease will necessarily be generated. Where there are two decks it is also more difficult to keep the men sufficiently exposed to the open atmosphere, as the idle and disobedient can more easily conceal themselves and remain below throughout the day.

"The difference in point of health is peculiarly striking between the troops conveyed in transports from England, and the slaves brought in the Guinea ships from Africa. Perhaps from the present mode of conducting slave ships might be derived some useful hints for the management of our transports. The slaves are much more crowded than the soldiers, yet far more healthy . . . I much suspect that it will be found in the difference in treatment and accommodation. According to the present method of conducting them, I might venture it as an opinion that a Guinea ship would carry — with much less danger of disease being generated among them — a cargo of slaves more than thrice as numerous as a transport would carry of soldiers.

". . . The nakedness of the slaves was perhaps their greatest security against disease. But in addition to their being without clothes, they are compelled to remain constantly upon deck in the day-time; and are encouraged to exercise and amusement. Their sleeping quarters are completedly washed out as soon as they quit them; and not species of baggage, nor clothing — not a bundle, nor any article of bedding — not even a single blanket, nor a sheet, nor any kind of thing that can create filth, or collect impurities is admitted.

"Hence it would seem that cleanliness, exercise, cheerfulness, a simple diet, and free exposure to the atmosphere are the greatest preventives of sickness — and that by a strict observance of these means the slaves make the voyage from Africa to the West Indies without engendering infectious maladies, although infinitely more crowded than troops on board even the most confined transport."

Dr. Pinckard attended the sale of a cargo of slaves from a Dutch ship at the new town of Amsterdam in the West Indies. It was a festive day, a kind of "public fair," he said, and he witnessed there the touching, near tragic incident involving a man's desperate attempt to keep his wife at his side.

"The belles and beaux appeared in their Sunday suits. Even the children were in full-dress, and their slaves decked out in holiday clothes . . . To the inhabitants it seemed a day of feasting and hilarity, but to the poor Africans it was a period of heavy grief and affliction; for they were to be sold as beasts of burden — torn from each other — and widely dispersed about the colony, to wear out their days in the hopeless toils of slavery.

"The fair being opened, and the crowd assembled, these un-pitied sable beings were exposed to the hammer of public auction. A long table was placed in the middle of a large room. At one end was seated the auctioneer, at the other was placed a chair for the Negroes to stand upon, in order to be exposed to the view of the purchasers; who were sitting at the sides of the table, or standing about the different parts of the room. All being in readiness, the slaves were brought in, one at a time, and placed upon the chair before the bidders, who handled and inspected them, with as little concern as if they had been examining cattle in Smithfield market. They turned them about, felt them, viewed their shapes and limbs, and looked into their mouths, made them jump and throw out their arms, and subjected them to all the means of trial as if dealing for a horse or other brute animal. Indeed the indelicacy shown towards the poor defenceless Africans, by some of these dealers in their species was not less unmanly and disgusting than it was insulting to humanity.

"We were shocked to observe women in the room who had come to the fair for the express purpose of purchasing slaves. Nay, even children were brought to point the lucky finger and the boy or girl, thus chosen, was bought by papa at the request of superstitious mama to give to young massa or missy.

"The price of these poor degraded blacks varied from 600 to 900 guilders, according to their age and strength, or their appearance being healthy or otherwise. The boys and girls were sold for 600 or 700 guilders. Some of the men fetched as high as 900 and the women were knocked down at about 800.

"In the course of the sale, a tall and robust Negro, on being brought into the auction room, approached the table with a fine Negress hanging upon his arm. The man was ordered to mount the chair. He obeyed, though manifestly with reluctance. His bosom heaved and grief was in his eye. The woman remained in the crowd. A certain price was mentioned to set the purchase forward, and the bidding commenced.

"But the slave, being desired to exhibit the activity of his limbs, and to display his person, sunk his chin upon his breast and hung his head in positive refusal. Then looking at the woman, he made signs expressive of great distress. Next, he pointed to her, and then to the chair, evidently intimating that he desired to have her placed by his side . . . Not obtaining immediate acquiescence, he became agitated and impatient. The sale was interrupted, and as he could not be prevailed upon to move a single muscle by way of exhibiting his person, the proceedings were at a stand. He looked again at the woman, again pointed to the chair, held up two fingers to the auctioneer, and implored the multitude in anxious suppliant gestures. Upon his countenance was marked the combined expressions of sorrow, affection and alarm. He grew more and more restless, and repeated signs which seemed to say — 'Let us be sold together.

Give me my heart's choice as the partner of my days, then dispose of me as you please, and I will be content to wear out my life in the heavy toils of bondage.'

"It was nature that spoke — and her language could not be mistaken. Humanity could no longer resist the appeal and it was universally agreed that they should make but one lot. A second chair was brought and the woman was placed at the side of her husband. His countenance instantly brightened. He hung upon the neck of his wife, and embraced her with rapture — then folding her in his arms, and pressing her to his bosom, he became composed, and looked round with a smile of complacency, which plainly said, 'Proceed — I am yours, yours, or yours! Let this be the associate of my toils, and I am satisfied.'

"The bidding was renewed. They exhibited marks of health and strength and quickly the two were sold together for 1650 guilders."

7

THE DOCTOR'S STORY

IN 1788, A BOOK entitled *An Account of the Slave Trade on the Coast of Africa* was published in England and it subsequently stirred an angry storm of opinion against the nation's participation in the business. The narration was authored by Dr. Alexander Falconbridge, based on his experiences as a surgeon aboard slave ships, and it provided a stark picture of the trade.

His descriptions of practices that were then current were corroborated again and again during Parliament's own investigations of the trade in 1789–91, by scores of witnesses called to testify, including captains, mates, sailors, merchants and other physicians.

Dr. Falconbridge himself became a victim of the African coast. His book and his stand on the slave trade won him popularity and favor of the abolitionists who were promoting a colony at Sierra Leone for freed slaves. He became the colony's governor, but after a short time lost the favor of his supporters and was fired. He took to drink and in a few weeks died.

We begin Dr. Falconbridge's story on the coast of Nigeria. The year is sometime in the early 1780's.

"The slave ships generally lie a mile below [Bonny and New Calabar] in Bonny river, in seven or eight fathoms of water.

Sometimes fifteen sail, English and French, but chiefly the former, meet here together. Soon after they cast anchor, the captains go on shore to make known their arrival and to inquire into the state of the trade. They likewise invite the kings of Bonny to come on board, to whom . . . they usually make presents (in that country termed dashes) which generally consist of pieces of cloth, cotton, chintz, silk handkerchiefs and other India goods and sometimes brandy, wine or beer.

"When I was at Bonny, a few years ago, it was the residence of two kings whose names were Norfolk and Peppel. The houses of these princes were not distinguished from the cottages or huts of which the town consists, in any other manner, than by being of somewhat larger dimensions and surrounded with warehouses containing European goods designed for the purchase of slaves. These slaves which the kings procured in the same manner as the black traders do theirs, are sold by them to the ships. And for every Negro sold there by the traders, the kings receive a duty which amounts to a considerable sum in the course of a year. This duty is collected by their officers stationed on board the ships . . .

"The kings of Bonny are absolute, though elective. They are assisted in the government by a small number of persons of a certain rank, who style themselves parliament gentlemen, an office which they generally hold for life. Every ship on its arrival, is expected to send a present to these gentlemen, of a small quantity of bread and beef, and likewise to treat them as often as they come on board. When they do this, their approach to the ship is announced by blowing through a hollow elephant's tooth which produces a sound resembling that of a post-horn.

"After the kings have been on board and have received the usual presents, permission is granted by them for trafficking with any of the black traders. When the royal guests return from the ships they are saluted by the guns.

"From the time of the arrival of the ships to their departure, which is usually about three months, scarce a day passes without some Negroes being purchased and carried on board; sometimes in small and sometimes in large numbers. The whole number taken on board depends on circumstances. In a voyage I once made, our stock of merchandise was exhausted in the purchase of about 380 Negroes, which was expected to have procured 500. The number of English and French ships then at Bonny had so far raised the price of Negroes as to occasion this difference.

"The reverse (and a happy reverse I think I may call it) was known during the late war [the American Revolution]. When I was last at Bonny, I frequently made inquiries on this head of one of the black traders whose intelligence I believe I can depend upon. He informed me that only one ship had been there for three years during that period; and that was the *Moseley Hill,* Captain Ewing, from Leverpool, who made an extraordinary purchase, as he found Negroes remarkably cheap from the dullness of trade. Upon further inquiring of my black acquaintance what was the consequence of this decay of their trade, he shrugged up his shoulders and answered, 'Only making us traders poorer and obliging us to work for our maintenance.' When one of these black merchants was informed that a particular set of people, called Quakers, were for abolishing the trade, he said it was a very bad thing, as they should be reduced to the same state they were in during the war, when, through poverty, they were obliged to dig the ground and plant yams.

"I was once upon the coast of Angola, also, when there had not been a slave ship at the river Ambris for five years previous to our arrival, although a place to which many usually resort every year. The failure of the trade for that period, as far as we could learn, had no other effect than to restore peace and confidence among the natives, which, upon the arrival of ships, is immediately destroyed by the inducement then held forth in the purchase of slaves. And during the suspension of trade at Bonny, as above-mentioned, none of the dreadful proceedings which are so confidently asserted to be the natural consequence, were known. The reduction of the price of Negroes and the poverty of the black traders appear to have been the only bad effects of the discontinuance of the trade; the good ones were most probably the restoration of peace and confidence among the natives and a suspension of kidnapping.

"After permission has been obtained for breaking trade, as it is termed, the captains go ashore, from time to time, to examine the Negroes that are exposed to sale and to make their purchases. The unhappy wretches thus disposed of are bought by the black traders at fairs, which are held for that purchase, at the distance of upwards of two hundred miles from the sea coast; and these fairs are said to be supplied from an interior part of the country. Many Negroes, upon being questioned relative to the places of their nativity, have asserted that they have travelled during the revolution of several moons (their usual method of calculating time) before they have reached the places where they were purchased by the black traders.

"At these fairs, which are held at uncertain periods, but generally every six weeks, several thousands are frequently exposed to sale who had been collected from all parts of the country for a very considerable distance around. . . . During one of my voyages, the black traders brought down, in different canoes, from twelve to fifteen hundred Negroes who had been purchased at one fair. They consisted chiefly of men and boys, the women seldom exceeding a third of the whole number. From forty to two hundred Negroes are generally purchased at a time by the black traders, according to the opulence of the buyer, and consist of all ages, from a month to sixty years and upwards. Scarcely any age or situation is deemed an exception, the price being proportionable. Women sometimes form a part of them, who happen to be so far advanced in their pregnancy as to be delivered during their journey from the fairs to the coast; and I have frequently seen instances of deliveries on board ship. The slaves purchased at these fairs are only for the supply of the markets at Bonny and Old and New Calabar.

"There is great reason to believe that most of the Negroes shipped from the coast of Africa are kidnapped. But the extreme care taken by the black traders to prevent the Europeans from gaining any intelligence of their modes of proceeding, the great distance inland from which the Negroes are brought, and our ignorance of their language (with which, very frequently, the black traders themselves are equally unacquainted) prevent our obtaining much information on this as we could wish. I have, however, by means of occasional inquiries made through interpreters, procured some intelligence relative to the point and such, as I think, puts the matter beyond a doubt.

"While I was employed on board one of the slave ships a Negro informed me that being one evening invited to drink with some of the black traders, they attempted to seize him as he was going away. As he was very active, he evaded them and got out of their hands. He was, however, prevented from effecting his escape by a large dog which laid hold of him and compelled him to submit. These creatures are kept by many of the traders for that purpose and being trained to the inhuman sport, they appear to be much pleased with it.

"I was likewise told by a Negro woman that as she was on her return home one evening, from some neighbors to whom she had been making a visit by invitation, she was kidnapped and notwithstanding she was big with child, she was sold for a slave. This transaction happened a considerable way up the country and she had passed through the hands of several purchasers before she reached the ship. A man and his son, according to their information, were seized by professed kidnappers, while they were planting yams, and sold for slaves. This also happened in the interior parts of the country; and after passing through several hands they were purchased for the ship to which I belonged.

"It frequently happens that those who kidnap others are themselves, in their turn, seized and sold. A Negro in the West Indies informed me that after being employed in kidnapping others he had experienced this reverse. And he assured me that it was a common incident among his countrymen.

"Continual enmity is thus fostered among the Negroes of Africa and all social intercourse between them destroyed; which most assuredly would not be the case had they not these opportunities for finding a ready sale for each other.

"During my stay on the coast of Africa, I was an eyewitness of the following transaction: — A black trader invited a Negro who resided a little way up the country, to come and see him. After the entertainment was over the trader proposed to his guest to treat him with a sight of one of the ships lying in the river. The unsuspicious countryman readily consented and accompanied the trader in a canoe to the side of the ship, which he viewed with pleasure and astonishment. While he was thus employed, some black traders on board, who appeared to be in on the secret, leaped into the canoe, seized the unfortunate man and dragging him into the ship immediately sold him.

"Previous to my being in this employ I entertained a belief, as many others have done, that the kings and principal men bred Negroes for sale as we do cattle. During the different times I was in the country, I took no little pains to satisfy myself in this particular; but notwithstanding I made many inquiries, I was not able to obtain the least intelligence of this being the case. . . . All the information I could procure confirms me in the belief that to kidnapping, and to crimes (and many of these fabricated as a pretext) the slave trade owes its chief support.

"The following instance tends to prove that artifice is often made use of. Several black traders, one of whom was a person of consequence and exercised an authority somewhat similar to that of our magistrates, being in want of some particular kind of merchandise and not having a slave to barter for it, they accused a fisherman with extortion in the sale of his fish; and as they were interested in the decision they immediately adjudged the poor fellow guilty and condemned him to be sold. He was accordingly purchased by the ship to which I belonged and brought on board.

"As an additional proof that kidnapping is not only the general but almost the sole mode by which slaves are procured, the black traders in purchasing them, choose those which are the roughest and most hardy; alleging that the smooth Negroes have been gentlemen. By this observation we may conclude they mean that nothing but fraud or force could have reduced these smooth-skinned gentlemen to a state of slavery.

"It may not be here unworthy to remark, in order to prove that the wars among the Africans do not furnish the number of slaves they are supposed to do, that I never saw any Negroes with recent wounds; which must have been the consequence, at least with some of them, had they been taken in battle. And it being my particular province, as the surgeon, to examine the slaves when they are purchased, such a circumstance could not have escaped my observation. As a further corroboration it might be remarked, that on the Gold and Windward Coasts, where fairs are not held, the number of slaves procured at a time are usually very small.

"The preparations made at Bonny by the black traders, upon setting out for the fairs which are held up the country, are very considerable. From twenty to thirty canoes, capable of containing thirty to forty Negroes each, are assembled for this purpose; and such goods put on board as they expect will be wanted for the purchase of the number of slaves they intend to buy. When their loading is completed they commence their voyage with colors flying and music playing and in about ten or eleven days generally return to Bonny with full cargoes. As soon as the canoes arrive at the trader's landing place, the purchased Negroes are cleaned and oiled with palm oil and on the following day they are exposed for sale to the captains.

"The black traders do not always purchase their slaves at the same rate. The speed with which the information of the arrival of ships upon the coast is conveyed to the fairs, considering that it is the interest of the traders to keep them ignorant, is really surprising. In a very short time after any ships arrive upon the coast, especially if several make their appearance together, those who dispose of the Negroes at the fairs are frequently known to increase the price of them. These fairs are not the only means, though they are the chief, by which the black traders on the coast are supplied with Negroes. Small parties of them, from five to ten, are frequently brought up to the houses of the traders, by those who make a practice of kidnapping and who are constantly employed in procuring a supply while purchasers are to be found.

"When the Negroes, whom the black traders have to dispose of, are shown to the European purchasers, they first examine them relative to their age. They then minutely inspect their persons and inquire into the state of their health; if they are afflicted with any disease or are deformed or have bad eyes or teeth; if they are lame or weak in the joints or distorted in the back or of a slender make or narrow in the chest; in short, if they have been ill or are afflicted in any manner so as to render them incapable of much labor. If any of the foregoing defects are discovered in them they are rejected. But if approved of, they are generally taken on board the ship the same evening. The purchaser has liberty to return on the following morning, but not afterwards, such as upon re-examination are found exceptionable.

"The traders frequently beat these Negroes which are objected to by the captains and use them with great severity. It matters not whether they are refused on account of age, illness, deformity or for any other reason. At New Calabar, in particular, the traders have frequently been known to put them to death. Instances have happened at that place, when Negroes have been objected to, that the traders have dropped their canoes under the stern of the vessel and instantly beheaded them in sight of the captain.

"Upon the Windward Coast another mode of procuring slaves is pursued; that is, by boating, a mode that is descriptive to the crews of the ships. The sailors who are employed upon this trade go in boats up the rivers, seeking for Negroes among the villages situated on the banks of these streams. But this method is very slow and not always effectual. After being absent from the ship during a fortnight or three weeks, they sometimes return with only eight to twelve Negroes . . .

"I have good reason to believe that of the one hundred and twenty Negroes purchased for the ship to which I then belonged, then lying at the river Ambris, by far the greater part, if not the whole, were kidnapped. This, with various other instances, confirms me in the belief that kidnapping is the fund that supplies the thousands of Negroes annually sold off the Windward and other coasts where boating prevails.

"On the arrival of the ships at Bonny and New Calabar, it is customary for them to unbend the sails, strike the yards and topmasts and begin to build what they denominate a house. The sailors first lash the booms and yards from mast to mast in order to form a ridge-pole. About ten feet above the deck, several spars, equal in length to the ridge-pole, are next lashed to the standing rigging and form a wall-plate. Across the ridge-pole and wallplate, several other spars or rafters are afterwards laid and lashed at the distance of about six inches from each other. On

these, other rafters or spars are laid lengthwise, equal in extent
to the ridge-pole, so as to form a kind of lattice or net-work, with
interstices of six inches square. The roof is then covered with
mats, made of rushes of very loose texture, fastened together
with rope-yarn and so placed as to lap over each other like
tiles . . .

"Near the mainmast a partition is constructed of boards which
reaches athwart the ship. This division is called a barricado. It is
about eight feet in height and is made to project about two feet
over the sides of the ship. In this barricado there is a door at
which a centinel is placed during the time the Negroes are permitted to come upon the deck. It serves to keep the different
sexes apart; and as there are small holes in it, where blunder-
busses are fixed and sometimes a cannon, it is found very convenient for quelling the insurrections that now and then happen.
Another door is made in the lattice or network at the ladder by
which you enter the ship. This door is guarded by a centinel during the day and is locked at night. At the head of the ship there is
a third door, for the use of the sailors, which is secured in the
same manner as that at the gangway. There is also in the roof a
large trap-door through which the goods intended for barter, the
water casks, and other such items are hoisted out or in.

"The design of this house is to secure those on board from the
heat of the sun, which in this latitude is intense, and from the
wind and rain which at particular seasons are likewise extremely
violent. It answers these purposes, however, but very ineffectu-
ally. The slight texture of the mats admits both the wind and the
rain, whenever it happens to be violent, though at the same time
it increases the heat of the ship to a very pernicious degree,
especially between decks. The increased warmth occasioned by
this means, together with the smoke produced from the green
mangrove (the usual firewood) which, for want of a current of
air to carry it off, collects and infests every part of the ship, ren-

der a vessel during its stay here very unhealthy. The smoke also, by its acrimonious quality, often produces inflammations in the eyes which terminates sometimes in the loss of sight.

"Another purpose for which these temporary homes are erected is to prevent the purchased Negroes from leaping overboard. This, the horrors of their situation frequently impel them to attempt; and they now and then effect it, notwithstanding all the precautions that are taken, by forcing their way through the lattice work.

"As soon as the wretched Negroes purchased at the fairs fall into the hands of the black traders, they experience in earnest the sufferings which they are doomed in future to undergo. There is not the least room to doubt that even before they can reach the fairs, great numbers perish from cruel usage, want of food and traveling through inhospitable deserts. They are brought from the places where they are purchased to Bonny, and the other slaving ports on the coastal rivers, in canoes, at the bottom of which they lie, having their hands tied with a kind of willow twig and a strict watch is kept over them. Their usage in other respects, during the time of the passage, which generally lasts several days, is equally cruel. Their allowance of food is so scanty that it is barely sufficient to support nature. They are, besides, much exposed to the violent rains which frequently fall, being covered only with mats that afford but a slight defence; and as there is usually water in the bottom on the canoes they are scarcely ever dry.

"Nor do these unhappy beings, after they become the property of the Europeans (from whom, as a more civilized people, more humanity might naturally be expected), find their situation in the least amended. Their treatment is no less rigorous. The men Negroes, on being brought aboard the ship, are immediately fastened together, two and two, by handcuffs on their wrists and by irons rivetted on their legs. They are then sent down between the

decks and placed in an apartment partitioned off for that purpose. The women also are placed in a separate apartment between decks, but without being ironed. An adjoining room on
the same deck is appointed for the boys. Thus they are all placed
in different apartments.

"But at the same time, however, they are frequently stowed so
close, as to admit of no other position than lying on their sides.
Nor will the height between decks, unless directly under the
grating, permit the indulgence of an erect posture; especially
where there are platforms, which is generally the case. These
platforms are a kind of shelf, about eight or nine feet in breadth,
extending from the side of the ship toward the centre. They are
placed nearly midway between the decks, at the distance of two
or three feet from each deck. Upon these the Negroes are stowed
in the same manner as they are on the deck underneath.

"In each of the apartments are placed three or four large
buckets, of a conical form, nearly two feet in diameter at the
bottom and only one foot at the top and in depth of about twenty-
eight inches, to which, when necessary, the Negroes have re-
course. It often happens that those who are placed at a distance
from the buckets, in endeavoring to get to them, tumble over
their companions, in consequence of their being shackled. These
accidents, although unavoidable, are productive of continual
quarrels in which some of them are always bruised. In this distressed situation, unable to proceed and prevented from getting
to the tubs, they desist from the attempt; and as the necessities
of nature are not to be resisted, ease themselves as they lie. This
becomes a fresh source of boils and disturbances and tends to
render the condition of the poor captive wretches still more un-
comfortable. The nuisance arising from these circumstances is
not infrequently increased by the tubs being much too small for
the purpose intended and their being usually emptied but once
every day. The rule for doing so, however, varies in different

ships according to the attention paid to the health and convenience of the slaves by the captain.

"About eight o'clock in the morning the Negroes are generally
brought upon deck. Their irons being examined, a long chain,
which is locked to a ring-bolt fixed in the deck, is run through the
rings of the shackles of the men and then locked to another ring-
bolt fixed also in the deck. By this means fifty or sixty and sometimes more are fastened to one chain in order to prevent them
from rising or endeavoring to escape. If the weather proves
favorable they are permitted to remain in that situation till four
or five in the afternoon when they are disengaged from the chain
and sent below.

"The diet of the Negroes while on board, consists chiefly of
horse beans boiled to the consistency of a pulp; of boiled yams
and rice and sometimes a small quantity of beef or pork. The
latter are frequently taken from the provisions laid in for the
sailors. They sometimes make use of a sauce composed of palm-
oil mixed with flour, water and pepper, which the sailors call
slabber-sauce. Yams are the favorite food of the Eboe or Bight
Negroes, and rice or corn of those from the Gold or Windward
Coast; each preferring the produce of their native soil.

"In their own country the Negroes in general live on animal
food and fish, with roots, yams and Indian corn. The horse beans
and rice, with which they are fed aboard ship, are chiefly taken
from Europe. The latter, indeed, is sometimes purchased on the
coast where it is superior to the other.

"The Gold Coast Negroes scarcely ever refuse any food that is
offered them and they generally eat larger quantities of whatever is placed before them than any other species of Negroes,
whom they also excell in strength of body and mind. Most of the
slaves have such an aversion to the horse beans that unless they
are narrowly watched, when fed upon the deck they will throw
them overboard or in each other's faces when they quarrel.

"They are commonly fed twice a day; about eight o'clock in the morning and four in the afternoon. In most ships they are only fed with their own food once a day. Their food is served up to them in tubs about the size of a small water bucket. They are placed round these tubs, in companies of ten to each tub, out of which they feed themselves with wooden spoons. These they soon lose and when they are not allowed others they feed themselves with their hands. In favorable weather they are fed upon deck but in bad weather their food is given them below. Numberless quarrels take place among them during their meals; more especially when they are put upon short allowance, which frequently happens if the passage from the coast of Guinea to the West Indies islands proves of unusual length. In that case, the weak are obliged to be content with a very scanty portion. Their allowance of water is about half a pint each at every meal. It is handed round in a bucket and given to each Negro in a pannekin, a small utensil with a straight handle, somewhat similar to a sauce-boat. However, when the ships approach the islands with a favourable breeze, the slaves are no longer restricted.

"Upon the Negroes refusing to take sustenance, I have seen coals of fire, glowing hot, put on a shovel and placed so near their lips as to scorch and burn them. And this has been accompanied with threats of forcing them to swallow the coals if they any longer persisted in refusing to eat. These means have generally had the desired effect. I have also been credibly informed that a certain captain in the slave-trade, poured melted lead on such of his Negroes as obstinately refused their food.

"Exercise being deemed necessary for the preservation of their health they are sometimes obliged to dance when the weather will permit their coming on deck. If they go about it reluctantly or do not move with agility, they are flogged; a person standing by them all the time with a cat-o'-nine-tails in his hand for that purpose. Their music, upon these occasions, consists of a drum, sometimes with only one head; and when that is worn out they make use of the bottom of one of the tubs before described. The poor wretches are frequently compelled to sing also; but when they do so, their songs are generally, as may naturally be expected, melancholy lamentations of their exile from their native country.

"The women are furnished with beads for the purpose of affording them some diversion. But this end is generally defeated by the squabbles which are occasioned in consequence of their stealing them from each other.

"On board some ships the common sailors are allowed to have intercourse with such of the black women whose consent they can procure. And some of them have been known to take the inconstancy of their paramours so much to heart as to leap overboard and drown themselves. The officers are permitted to indulge their passions among them at pleasure and sometimes are guilty of such excesses as disgrace human nature.

"When the ships have disposed of all of their merchandise in the purchase of Negroes and have laid in their stock of wood, water, and yams, they prepare for sailing by getting up the yards and topmasts, reeving the running rigging, bending the sails, and by taking down the temporary house. They then drop down the river to wait for a favorable opportunity to pass over the bar which is formed by a number of sand banks lying across the mouth of the river, with navigable channels between them. It is not uncommon for ships to get up the bar and sometimes they are lost.

"The hardships and inconveniences suffered by the Negroes during the passage are scarcely to be enumerated or conceived. They are far more violently affected by seasickness than Europeans. It frequently terminates in death, especially among the women. But the exclusion of fresh air is among the most intolerable. For the purpose of admitting this needful refreshment, most of the ships in the slave trade are provided, between the decks, with five or six air-ports on each side of the ship, of about five inches in length and four in breadth. In addition, some ships, but not one in twenty, have what they denominate wind-sails. But whenever the sea is rough and the rain heavy it becomes necessary to shut these and every other conveyance by which the air is admitted. The fresh air being thus excluded, the Negroes' rooms soon grow intolerable hot. The confined air, rendered noxious by the effluvia exhaled from their bodies and being repeatedly breathed, soon produces fevers and fluxes which generally carries off great numbers of them.

"During the voyages I made, I was frequently witness to the fatal effects of this exclusion of fresh air. I will give one instance, as it serves to convey some idea, though a very faint one, of their terrible sufferings. . . . Some wet and blowing weather having occasioned the port-holes to be shut and the grating to be covered, fluxes and fevers among the Negroes ensued. While they were in this situation, I frequently went down among them till at length their room became so extremely hot as to be only bearable for a very short time. But the excessive heat was not the only thing that rendered their situation intolerable. The deck, that is the floor of their rooms, was so covered with the blood and mucus which had proceeded from them in consequence of the flux, that it resembled a slaughter-house. It is not in the power of the human imagination to picture a situation more dreadful or disgusting. Numbers of the slaves having fainted, they were carried upon deck where several of them died and the rest with great difficulty were restored. It had nearly proved fatal to me also. The climate was too warm to admit the wearing of any clothing but a shirt and that I had pulled off before I went down. . . . In a quarter of an hour I was so overcome with the heat, stench and foul air that I nearly fainted, and it was only with assistance I could get back on deck. The consequence was that I soon after fell sick of the same disorder from which I did not recover for several months.

"A circumstance of this kind sometimes repeatedly happens in the course of a voyage; and often to a greater degree than that which has just been described, particularly when the slaves are much crowded, which was not the case at the time, the ship having more than a hundred short of the number she was to have taken in.

"This devastation, great as it was, some years ago was greatly exceeded by a Leverpool ship . . . This ship, though a much smaller ship than in which I have just mentioned, took on board at Bonny at least six hundred Negroes . . . By purchasing so great a number, the slaves were so crowded that they were obliged to lie one upon another. This caused such a mortality among them that without meeting with unusually bad weather or having a longer voyage than common, nearly one half of them died before the ship arrived in the West Indies.

"That the public may be able to form some idea of the almost incredibly small space into which so large a number of Negroes were crammed, the following particulars of this ship are given. According to Leverpool custom she measured 235 tons. Her width across the beam, 25 feet. Length between the decks, 92 feet, which was divided into four rooms, thus:

Store room, in which there were not any Negroes placed	15 feet
Negroes' rooms: men's rooms — about	45 feet
women's rooms — about	10 feet
boys' rooms — about	22 feet
Total room for Negroes	77 feet

"Exclusive of the platform before described, from 8 to 9 feet in breadth, and equal in length to that of the rooms.

"It may be worthy of remark, the ships in this trade are usually fitted out to receive only one third women Negroes, or perhaps a smaller number, which the dimensions of the room allotted for them, above given, plainly show but in a greater disproportion.

"One would naturally suppose that an attention to their own interest would prompt the owners of the Guinea ships not to suffer the captains to take on board a greater number of Negroes than the ship would allow sufficient room for them to lie with ease to themselves, or, at least, without rubbing against each other. However that may be, a more striking instance than the above, of avarice, completely and deservedly disappointed, was surely never displayed, for there is little room to doubt but that in consequence of that expected premium usually allowed to the captains of 6 pounds per cent sterling on the produce of the Negroes, this vessel was so crowded as to occasion such a heavy loss.

"The place allotted for the sick Negroes is under the half deck, where they lie on the bare planks. By this means those who are emaciated frequently have their skin and even their flesh entirely rubbed off, by the motion of the ship, from the prominent parts of the shoulders, elbows and hips so as to render the bones quite bare.

"And some of them, by constantly lying in the blood and mucus that had flowed from those afflicted with the flux and which is generally so violent as to prevent their being kept clean, having their flesh much sooner rubbed off than those who have only to contend with the mere friction of the ship. The excruciating pain which the poor sufferers feel from being obliged to continue in such a dreadful situation, frequently for several weeks, in case they happen to live so long, is not to be conceived or described. Few, indeed, are able to withstand the fatal effects of it. The utmost skill of the surgeon is here ineffectual. If plasters are applied they are very soon displaced by the friction of the ship, and when bandages are used the Negroes soon take them off and appropriate them to other purposes.

"The surgeon, upon going between the decks in the morning to examine the situation of the slaves, frequently finds several dead, and among the men, sometimes a dead and living Negro fastened together by their irons. When this is the case they are brought upon the deck and being laid on the grating, the living Negro is disengaged and the dead one thrown overboard.

"It may not be improper here to remark that the surgeons employed in the Guinea trade are generally driven to engage in so disagreeable an employment by the confined state of their finances. An exertion of the greatest skill and attention could afford the diseased Negroes little relief so long as the causes of their disease, namely the breathing of a putrid atmosphere and wallowing in their excrements remain. When once the fever and dysentery get to any height at sea, a cure is scarcely ever effected.

"Almost the only means by which the surgeon can render himself useful to the slaves is by seeing that their food is properly cooked and distributed among them. It is true, when they arrive near the markets for which they are destined, care is taken to polish them for sale by an application of the lunar caustic to such as afflicted with the yaws. This, however, affords but a temporary relief as the disease most assuredly breaks out whenever the Negro is put upon a vegetable diet.

"It has been asserted, in favor of the captains in the trade, that the sick slaves are usually fed from their tables. The great number generally ill at a time proves the falsity of such an assertion. Were a captain even disposed to do this, how could he feed half the slaves in the ship from his own table? For it is well known that more than half are often sick at a time. Two or three perhaps may be fed.

"This loss of slaves, through mortality, arising from the causes just mentioned is frequently very considerable. One half, sometimes two thirds and even beyond that have been known to perish. Before we left the Bonny River, no less than fifteen died of fevers and dysenteries occasioned by their confinement. On the Windward Coast, where slaves are procured more slowly, very few die in proportion to the numbers which die at Bonny and at Old and New Calabar where they are obtained much faster, the latter being of a more delicate make and habit.

"As very few of the Negroes can so far brook the loss of their liberty and the hardships they endure, they are ever on the watch to take advantage of the least negligence in their oppressors. Insurrections are frequently the consequence; which are seldom expressed without much bloodshed. Sometimes these are successful and the whole ship's company is cut off. They are likewise always ready to seize every opportunity for committing some acts of desperation to free themselves from their miserable state and notwithstanding the restraints which are laid, they often succeed.

"While a ship to which I belonged lay in Bonny River, one evening a short time before our departure a lot of Negroes, consisting of about ten, were brought on board. One of them in a favorable moment forced his way through the network on the larboard side of the vessel, jumped overboard and was supposed to have been devoured by the sharks. During the time we were there, fifteen Negroes belonging to a vessel from Leverpool found means to throw themselves into the river. Very few were saved and the residue fell a sacrifice to the sharks . . .

"Circumstances of this kind are very frequent. On the coast of Angola, at the River Ambris, the following incident happened: — During the time of our residing on shore we erected a tent to shelter ourselves from the weather. After having been there several weeks and being unable to purchase the number of slaves we wanted, through the opposition of another English slave vessel, we determined to leave the place. The night before our departure the tent was struck, which was no sooner perceived by some of the Negro women on board than it was considered a prelude to

our sailing and about eighteen of them, when they were sent between decks, threw themselves into the sea through one of the
gun ports, the ship carrying guns between decks. They were all
of them, however, excepting one, soon picked up, and that which
was missing was not long after taken about a mile from the shore.

"The following circumstance also came within my knowledge.
A young female Negro, falling into a desponding way, it was
judged necessary in order to attempt her recovery to send her on
shore to the hut of one of the black traders. Elated with the
prospect of regaining her liberty, she soon recovered her usual
cheerfulness. But hearing by accident, that she was to be taken
on board the ship again, the poor young creature hung herself.

"It frequently happens that the Negroes on being purchased by
Europeans, become raving mad and many of them die in that
state, particularly the women. One day at Bonny I saw a middle-
aged, stout woman who had been brought down from a fair the
day before, chained to the post of a black trader's door in a state
of furious insanity. On board a ship in Bonny River, I saw a
young Negro woman chained to the deck, who had lost her senses
soon after she was purchased and taken on board. In a former
voyage we were obliged to confine a female Negro of about
twenty-three years of age on her becoming a lunatic. She was
afterwards sold during one of her lucid intervals.

"One morning upon examining the places allotted for the sick
Negroes, I perceived that one of them, who was so emaciated as
scarcely to be able to walk, was missing and was convinced that
he must have gone overboard in the night, probably to put a more
expeditious end to his sufferings.

"When the ships arrive in the West Indies (the chief mart for
this inhuman merchandize), the slaves are disposed as I have
before observed by different methods. Sometimes the mode of
disposal is that of selling them by what is termed a scramble,
and a day is soon fixed for that purpose. Previously the sick or

refuse slaves, of which there are frequently many, are usually conveyed on shore and sold at a tavern, by vendue or public auction. These, in general, are purchased . . . upon speculation, at so low a price as five or six dollars a head. I was informed by a mulatto woman that she purchased a sick slave at Grenada, upon speculation, for the small sum of one dollar, as the poor wretch was apparently dying of the flux. It seldom happens that any who are carried ashore in the emaciated state to which they are generally reduced by that disorder long survive after their landing. I once saw sixteen conveyed on shore and sold in the foregoing manner, the whole of whom died before I left the island. Sometimes the captains march their slaves through the town at which they intend to dispose of them, and then place them in rows where they are examined and purchased.

"The mode of selling them by scramble having fallen under my observation the oftenest, I shall be more particular in describing it. Being some years ago, at one of the islands in the West Indies, I was witness to a sale by scramble, where about 250 Negroes were sold. Upon this occasion all the Negroes scrambled for bear an equal price; which is agreed upon between the captains and the purchasers before the sale begins. On a day appointed, the Negroes were landed and placed together in a large yard belonging to the merchants to whom the ship was consigned. As soon as the hour agreed on arrived, the doors of the yard were suddenly thrown open and in rushed a considerable number of purchasers, with all the ferocity of brutes. Some instantly seized such of the Negroes as they could conveniently lay hold of with their hands. Others being prepared with several handkerchiefs tied together, encircled as many as they were able. While others, by means of a rope, effected the same purpose. It is scarcely possible to describe the confusion of which this mode of selling is productive. It likewise causes much animosity among the purchasers who not infrequently fall out and quarrel with each other. The poor astonished Negroes were so terrified by these proceedings, that several of them, through fear climbed over the walls of the courtyard and ran wild about the town, but were soon hunted down and retaken.

"While on a former voyage from Africa to Kingston in Jamaica, I saw a sale there by scramble on board a snow.* The Negroes were collected together upon the main and quarter decks and the ship was darkened by sails suspended over them in order to prevent the purchasers from being able to see, so as to pick and choose. The signal being given, the buyers rushed in, as usual, to seize their prey. The Negroes appeared to be extremely terrified and nearly thirty of them jumped into the sea. But they were soon retaken, chiefly by boats from other ships.

"On board a ship lying at Port Maria, in Jamaica, I saw another scramble in which, as usual, the Negroes were greatly terrified. The women, in particular, clung to each other, shrieking in terror at the savage manner in which their brutal purchasers rushed upon them and seized them.

"Various deceptions are used in the disposal of sick slaves and many of these must excite in every humane mind the liveliest sensations of horror. I have been well informed that a Leverpool captain boasted of his having cheated some Jews by the following stratagem. A lot of slaves afflicted with the flux, being about to be landed for sale, he directed the ship's surgeons to stop the anus of each of them with oakum. Thus prepared they were landed and taken to the accustomed place of sale, where, being unable to stand but for a very short time, they were usually permitted to sit. The buyers, when they examine them, oblige them to stand up in order to see if there be any discharge; and when they do not perceive this appearance they consider it as a symptom of recovery. In the present instance, such an appearance being prevented, the bargain was struck and the slaves were accordingly

* A type of brig.

sold. But it was not long before discovery ensued. The excruciating pain which the prevention of a discharge of such an acrimonious nature occasioned, not being able to be borne by the poor
wretches, the temporary obstruction was removed and the deluded purchasers were speedily convinced of the imposition."

8

CAPTAIN HUGH CROW
OUT OF LIVERPOOL

Nearly every port on the North Atlantic sent out slave ships at one time or another, but the English slaving ports of London, then Bristol and finally Liverpool achieved the greatest infamy by their participation.

London led the commerce first, and was the principal port for English slavers for many years. It was also the financial center for such ventures and the headquarters of the Royal African Company, which was given monopoly slave shipping rights by the crown.

But when the English trade was thrown open to all venturers at the end of the seventeenth century, Bristol took the trade away from London because it was closer to the places that manufactured the goods used in the trade for slaves. With the advent of the industrial revolution, England coupled its commerce very largely to supplying the Guinea Coast with its products, in exchange for the African coast's chief commodity — slaves.

In the early years of the eighteenth century, Bristol and Liverpool vied for the African market, and the parsimonious Liverpool merchants won. They ignored the traditional methods of financing slave voyages and set their own rules. Instead of paying ship captains and coast traders on commission, the Liverpool merchants put them on straight salaries. Captains' shipboard privileges were trimmed considerably. Apprentice boys instead of trained seamen were hired at lower rates to make up most of the crew, and the crews were reduced to a minimum to save money. The latter practice boomeranged occasionally, however, since the smaller crews were easy prey to slave uprisings and Liverpool ships experienced far more revolts than those from other ports.

At first, Liverpool was not able to afford to gamble on the slave trade. Instead, it got into a successful competition with Bristol and European ports in exports to the West Indies and the American colonies. Its Manchester textiles soon proved popular with the New World residents, who preferred them to the more expensive, often inferior goods offered by others. In American stores, Manchester checks soon were replacing the German, French and Scotch osnaburgs exported from Bristol.

To protect their own manufacturing sources, which paid the customary levies, the Spaniards sought to stop the traffic of Manchester goods to their West Indian colonies. Sloops and sailing canoes from the Spanish islands were found to be making the long trip to Jamaica to make purchases of Liverpool wares and smuggle them home for resale. In 1739, the Spanish Guarda Costa — the Caribbean sea police — seized an English ship and sliced off an ear of the captain, Robert Jenkins. As proof of the intrusion, the Spanish shipped Jenkins's ear back to Europe in a bottle. The act precipitated a war between England and Spain that lasted for two years, but it stopped the smuggling.

Liverpool at that point, however, had the financial resources it needed for the far more profitable Guinea slave trade. It soon outdistanced every competitor, and by the end of the century had won the distinction of being the chief slaving town in the Old World.

As one critic remarked, Liverpool carried on its commerce in ebony with a vitality worthy of a far better cause. Nearly everyone became involved in some way or another. Small shop owners, barbers, street vendors purchased shares in a slaving enterprise. All the great families were steeped in the business. Shops and storefronts displayed leg-irons, handcuffs and other implements necessary for a slaving voyage. Faster and larger ships were built at Liverpool and fitted to carry the slaves. Across its docks and into the ships' holds went woolen goods from Manchester and Yorkshire and hatchets, cutlasses, knives, gunpowder, trinkets, pistols and muskets from Birmingham and Sheffield. The town's populace for the most part looked on slave shipping with no more scruples than if their ships had been hauling cattle.

In 1730 there were only fifteen small ships in the Liverpool fleet. By 1751 there were fifty-three, with a total tonnage of 5,334. By 1792, the fleet had grown to one hundred thirty-six slave ships with a total of 24,544 tons burden. By 1795, better than 60 percent of the entire English slave commerce was carried in Liverpool vessels.*

Other nations were also deeply involved in the trade, but were not capable of going to such lengths as the Englishmen. In 1784, one estimate had it that seventy-four thousand slaves were shipped annually across the Atlantic in European vessels — with four thousand carried by the Dutch, ten thousand by Portuguese, two thousand by Danes, twenty thousand by the French, and thirty-eight thousand by the English.

From 1783 to 1793, it was estimated that Liverpool ships carried more than three hundred thousand slaves for gross slave sales of £15,186,850.*

Just what were the profits? They could, of course, vary from voyage to voyage, depending on conditions on the coast of Africa, in the West Indies, what European nations were at war, and a variety of other factors. One account broke down the figures for

* Gomer Williams, *The Liverpool Privateers*. London, 1897.

Liverpool for the year 1786, a fairly good period of slave trading for the port. The port shipped and sold a total of 31,690 slaves that year for £1,282,690. It cost £864,895 for the goods to buy them, £103,488 in shipping costs and £15,845 in slave maintenance — food, handling — to make a net profit of £298,462. This represented a net gain of slightly less than £10 per slave.*

The wealth that came to the port of Liverpool dazzled its residents, blinding them to any thoughts on the morality of the business. Since the livelihood of nearly everyone in the city was so closely tied to the traffic, any threat to it was something to be promptly put down.

When the abolitionists began stirring up sentiment to end the trade, petitions signed by the thousands of Liverpool residents were sent to Parliament in opposition. Those scant brave souls who sided with the reformers were scorned and ostracized. When Parliament rang down the curtain on the trade in 1807, there arose a great wail of distress that ruin had finally come.

Therefore it was not wholly coincidental that the *Kitty's Amelia*, the last English slave ship to leave the nation legally, sailed from Liverpool. Her captain was Hugh Crow, one of Liverpool's most acclaimed slave ship commanders. Crow was one of the most voluble and colorful persons of his calling and it's unlikely that history could have picked a better narrator to describe this voyage marking the end of an era.

Crow was a Manxman — a native of the Isle of Man in the Irish Sea — and was proud of it. He went to sea and became one of the nation's better captains, never lacking for commands because of his sailing skill and ability to keep losses low. Early in life he lost an eye, and the piercing glance of the other won him the nickname of "Mind Your Eye Crow." He was a fighter and built up a reputation for scrappiness when challenged. Once in

---

* *Liverpool and Slavery, an Historical Account of the Liverpool-African Slave Trade.* Liverpool, 1884.

the 1780's, as chief mate of a Guinea ship, Crow was captured with the rest of the crew by a French man-of-war. The Englishmen were imprisoned in Brittany and were allowed to starve except for the food and money sent by friends in England. Many of his shipmates and other English seamen imprisoned with them died in the following months, but Crow doggedly held on to life. He was marched across France to another jail where he arrived feverish, footsore and exhausted. The determined Crow then escaped and walked back across France at night by himself, knowing little of his captors' language. At Le Havre, he gained passage aboard a Danish vessel back to England and freedom, arriving with little more than a firm resolve that his capture would be a great deal more costly to his enemy the next time.

Not long afterwards Crow was given command of the *Mary*, a vessel heavily armed with cannon to fight its way to and from the Guinea Coast and the West Indies. The times were tense between England and France and no ship passed unchallenged by the men-of-war of either nation. Soon after the *Mary* sailed, two British warships overtook her and attempted to outflank her. Though he could see his pursuers flying the British ensign, as they could see his, Crow feared trickery and immediately opened fire, which the warships just as quickly returned. The fight went on fiercely into the night. In the dawn light, Crow was wounded slightly and fell unconscious. When he came to he found the crew had struck the *Mary*'s colors and the attackers were boarding her. They soon proved to be British. The commanders of the men-of-war exonerated Crow from any blame, however, and praised his ship's gallantry.

As a captain, Crow prided himself on his treatment of his slave cargoes. He was reportedly one of the few who taught slaves to shoot and used them in times of attack to help repel the enemy. Crow said he never had to regret the practice; the entrusted slaves always proved their loyalty despite the loaded guns in their hands. He was not above boastful self-praise, but then few captains knew the full meaning of modesty. In his autobiography, written some years after he retired, Crow recalls one morning at Kingston, Jamaica; he was lying on his bunk in his cabin when his chief mate hurried in to tell him that a " 'great number of black men and women have come aboard, all dressed in their best and they are anxious to see you — will you allow them to come down?'*

" 'By all means,' " said Crow, springing up and hastily putting on his clothes. "In a moment they all rushed into the cabin and crowding round me with gestures of respect, and with tears in their eyes, exclaimed, 'God bless massa. How poor massa do? Long live massa, for im da fight ebery voyage,' and similar expressions of good will and welcome. I soon recognized these kind creatures as having been with me in one or other of the actions in which I had been engaged on former voyages, and though my attention to them, when on board, was no more than I had always considered proper and humane, I was deeply affected by this mark of their grateful remembrance.

"Poor Scott [the mate] shed tears when he saw them clinging round me and observed, 'How proud, sir, you must be to receive this grateful tribute of regard. And how few captains can boast of a similar proof of their good treatment of the blacks under their charge.' Indeed, I could not refrain from shedding tears myself, when I reflected that the compliment came from poor creatures whom I had brought from their homes on the coast of Africa. The women were neatly dressed in calicoes and muslins; their hair was tastefully arranged, and they wore long gold earrings. The men appeared in white shirts and trowsers and flash neck-cloths, with their hair neatly plaited. The whole were at once clean and cheerful, and I was glad from my heart to see them. When they left the ship, which was not until they had repeatedly

* Williams, *Liverpool Privateers*.

expressed their happiness to see me again, I distributed amongst them a sum of money, and they bade me good-bye, with hearts full of thankfulness and joy."

Crow returned from one voyage in the spring of 1807 and immediately was engaged as commander of the *Kitty's Amelia*. The end of the slave trade had been declared by Parliament to be effective May 1, but the owner of the *Kitty's Amelia* had gotten the ship's articles cleared before that time. Though the three hundred-ton, eighteen-gun vessel did not actually set sail until July 27, 1807, nearly three months after the deadline, her voyage was still legal. The underwriters also bestowed on Crow the highest praise they could give a skipper and insured the cargo on terms 5 percent lower than was customary.

But despite Crow's good record, the voyage of the *Kitty's Amelia* was destined to ill luck. Though she sailed with navy agreements that her crew would not be subject to impressment, the *Kitty's Amelia* was only a few days from port when a navy frigate pulled alongside and took four of Crow's best seamen. Crow, like most merchant ship captains, despised the navy's long-held privilege of impressing those sailors it felt it needed from any English ship it came across.

On an earlier voyage, the frigate *Amethyst* had taken a number of his seamen and Crow later wrote, "The impressment of these men by a frigate which I have ascertained was full of men, was nothing less than a robbery of our merchants on the high seas by parties from whom we had a right to look for protection. This was not, however, the only instance in which the merchant service, from which the riches of the state and her best defence are derived, was wantonly crippled and distressed, and that our merchants tamely suffered themselves to be so much oppressed is only to be accounted for on the supposition that no general effort was resorted to, to counteract the grievance."

When the *Kitty's Amelia* reached the Bonny River, in the early fall of 1807, a dozen other ships were also waiting for slaves. King Holiday, the chief, immediately rowed out to see Crow. Why, he asked the Manxman, was the trade being stopped by Crow's country? It was profitable and the white men seemed to sail away as happy as when they came, the chief noted wistfully. They talked a long time, King Holiday trying to discern some reason in it. If the white men could rid themselves of undesirables by shipping them to the African Coast, the king asked Crow, why should he be prevented from getting rid of the rogues of his land. And if the trade were to end, the king continued, many children would be killed because their parents couldn't support them.

" 'Crow, you and me sabby each other long time, and me know you tell me true mouth, for all captains come to river tell me you king and you big mans stop we trade, and 'spose dat true, what we do?' " Crow wrote that he could give the king no satisfactory answer for his countrymen's actions, for Crow — like so many others of Liverpool — regarded the trade as a necessary evil.

According to Crow, the king left in tears, whether for children he expected to die or for the pinch on his own purse, Crow didn't elaborate.

Trade in the Bonny River while the *Kitty's Amelia* was there was slow at first and then, after a lapse of several weeks, began to pick up. But the delay had been unfortunate for Crow. Sickness had broken out and, in addition, much of his goods for trade were found to be spoiled.

"Unfortunately, for us, in the hurry and bustle of fitting out the vessel at Liverpool, that she might be ready for sea before the passing of the bill abolishing the slave trade, a quantity of goods that had been returned on her former voyage (when the ship was sickly) had been carelessly repacked without drying or airing in damp water casks. And these were no sooner reopened than a malignant fever and dysentery broke out amongst the crew. The first man who died was a fine promising young man, Mr. Ray, our second mate. The sickness continued to rage amongst both whites and blacks. The goods being found to be almost rotten, we were obliged to give them away or throw them overboard. The loss of these articles of trade, together with the sickly state of the crew, tended to retard the purchase of our cargo, and my mind became in consequence much harassed and depressed. To add to our trouble the weather was extremely precipitous. We had, at intervals, some of the most awful thunder and lightning, attended by heavy rains, I ever witnessed; and one night in particular such was the concussion produced by the explosion of the electric fluid that the ship actually shook from stem to stern like a basket."

Crow finally got together a load of slaves which he noted was "as fine a cargo of blacks as had ever been taken from Africa."

This favorable news was probably the last Crow would record on the voyage. While en route to Saint Thomas, the island stopover on the path to the West Indies frequently used by slavers, many of Crow's slaves sickened. Storms and calms prolonged their miseries and beyond Saint Thomas, seamen and slaves died daily. Crow's luck ebbed further. Halfway across the Atlantic, the ship caught fire.

"I was in the cabin at the time and springing on deck, the first persons I saw were two young men with their flannel shirts blazing on their backs. At the same time I perceived a dense cloud of smoke issuing from below, and looking round me I found the people in the act of cutting away the stern and quarter boats that they might abandon the vessel. At this critical juncture I had the presence of mind to exclaim in an animating tone, 'Is it possible, my lads, that you can desert me at a moment when it is your bounden duty as men to assist me.'

"And observing them to hesitate, I added, 'Follow me, my brave fellows, and we shall soon save the ship.' These few words had the desired effect, for they immediately rallied and came forward to assist me. To show them a proper example I was the first man to venture below, for I thought of the poor blacks entrusted to my care and who could not be saved in the boats, and I was determined, rather than desert them, to extinguish the fire or perish in the attempt.

"When we got below we found the fire blazing with great fury on the starboard side, and as it was known to the crew that there [were] forty-five barrels of gunpowder in the magazine, within about three feet only of the fire, it required every possible encouragement on my part to lead them on to endeavour to extinguish the rapidly increasing flames. When I first saw the extent of the conflagration, and thought of its proximity to the powder, a thrill of despair ran through my whole frame; but by a strong mental effort I suppressed my disheartening feelings, and only thought of active exertion, unconnected with thought of imminent danger.

"We paused for a moment, struggling, as it were, to determine where to proceed. Very fortunately for us our spare sails were stowed close at hand. These were dragged out and by extraordinary activity we succeeded in throwing them over the flames which they so far checked that we gained time to obtain a good supply of water down the hatchway and in the course of ten or fifteen minutes, by favour of Almighty God, we extinguished the flames . . . The accident, I found, was occasioned by the ignorance and carelessness of the two young men whose clothes I had seen burning on their backs. Through the want of regular officers, they had been entrusted to draw off some rum from the store cask and not knowing the danger to which they exposed themselves and the ship, had taken a lighted candle, a spark from which had ignited the spirits . . ."

Nearly two months after leaving Saint Thomas, the *Kitty's Amelia* arrived at Kingston. Fifty slaves and thirty seamen had died in the voyage. Crow was dejected. He had a reputation of running a clean ship and the deaths depressed him. In addition, the harbor was crowded with slave ships and the market was glutted.

The ship's agents, however, advertised the cargo, and perhaps on the basis of Crow's record of providing good slaves, the cargo he had just brought sold at a higher price than those already there.

The *Kitty's Amelia* returned to Liverpool, but under the command of another captain. The despondent Crow returned to England six months later as a passenger on another ship and then retired to his native Isle of Man on the savings made during his seafaring days.

9

A "LAST" SLAVING VOYAGE

THE *Thomas Watson*, A FOUR HUNDRED-TON SHIP, was fitted in the spring of 1860 at New London, Connecticut, ostensibly for a three-year whaling voyage. She sailed first to New York for a crew and one of the seamen signed aboard there was Edward Manning, under the name of Edward Melville. His story is an interesting complement to that of Captain Phillips's in Chapter 4. Most of the crew, including Manning, were not told of the real purpose of the voyage — to haul slaves from Guinea to Cuba. But they suspected something. The ship was too clean to be a whaler and did not have the pervading smell of oil that clung about a legitimate whale ship. The *Thomas Watson* sailed from New York harbor in June 1860, on the voyage related by Manning in his book, *Six Months on a Slaver*, written shortly after his return.*

There were a number of "last" slave ship voyages before the Civil War ended the traffic, and although there is little to authenticate which voyage was actually the last, it can be said that the voyage Manning took on the *Thomas Watson* was one of the final ones of the trade. Slave shipping from Africa to the Western Hemisphere had been banned by the major nations for many

* Published New York, 1879.

years. The peril of impending seizure by one of the many naval cruisers which patrolled both the African coast, the American coast and the West Indies on the lookout for any "blackbirding" was the same for all these "last" slavers. The voyage of the *Thomas Watson* is presented here in the words of Manning as an example of one of the last slaving ventures, and as a sea adventure as well.

When the "whaler" reached the latitude of the Azores, lookouts were posted to spot "blows" of whales, a sham which was kept up until the ship reached the African coast. Manning tells the rest:

"It was not until we had done with cruising off the Azores Islands and had taken our departure for other parts, that our suspicions were aroused that the whaling business was merely a blind. The first evidence came to light after the crew had been set to working breaking out the hold, and it appeared in the shape of huge quantities of rice, hard-tack, salt beef, pork, etc., in quantities large enough to feed a regiment for a long time. We also found a great amount of light pine flooring. For what purpose it was intended we could not then imagine, but it will be seen, later on, that this was a very useful part of our outfit. The ship had no regular 'between-decks.' A small deck had been built directly under the main-hatch and it was called the 'blubber-room.' The blubber was supposed to be sent there for 'mincing.'

"For weeks the sham of whaling was carried on and, whenever a blow was cried out from aloft, all boats were called away. The master of a bona fide whaler could not have been more anxious to secure his fish than our captain appeared to be. The strict discipline of a whaler was also kept up and no favours had been shown in the way of grub. We still had only our allowance of salt beef, pork, hard-tack, and beans.

"Up to this time, however, we had not achieved much as a whaler, two or three porpoises being the net catch of fish, and they were harpooned from the bow. The blubber was stripped from them, after being minced and tried out, yielded but an insignificant quantity of oil — not enongh to make the try-pots even smell oily.

"When not in the boats the work of breaking out the hold still went on with vigor. After a large quantity of rice and hard-bread had been shifted to the lazaret, the other stores were stowed up even with the deck of the blubber-room. This was about five feet below the main deck. The pine flooring, which aroused our curiosity when it first came to light, was now laid smoothly down on top of the stores, thereby making a fair-looking floor. When we commenced breaking out the forward part of the hold it was found to contain chiefly large oil casks filled with fresh water. After stowing them in a like manner as we had done the stores, namely, even with the blubber-room, we laid the pine flooring on top of them, and then had a smooth floor, fore and aft. This was the second tangible piece of evidence that our 'whales' would not be taken out of the 'mighty ocean.'

"The crew generally seemed to be well pleased at the new phase the voyage had taken and were anxious for the time to come when the ship would be well filled with 'blackfish' oil, as they termed the Negroes, and her bow pointed toward the States. I did not share in their satisfaction at the changed aspects of affairs, for I had scruples about being made an outlaw in this summary manner and I foolishly expressed my sentiments openly. I thus brought on myself the ill-will of the captain. Later on, after the voyage was ended and while I was waiting for a passage in a Mexican schooner from Campeachy, Yucatan, to New Orleans, he swore that I should never leave the beach alive. This, however, was all brag. I knew him to be a coward and it did not intimidate me in the least.

"Nearly three months had passed since we took our departure

from Sandy Hook and during all that time, with the exception of breaking out the hold, there had been nothing unusual to change the monotonous routine of daily work. But I judged now, by the whitish appearance of the water and the orders given to the look-out to 'keep his eyes wide open,' that we must be approaching land. The captain also passed a large part of the time on deck, night and day, and whenever a sail was reported from aloft, he would jump into the rigging, spy-glass in hand, and intently watch the approach of the stranger. If the course she was sailing would bring her within hailing distance, we at once avoided her by changing our course. Two or three times the skippers of different vessels manifested a desire to communicate with us by following in our wake, but, our ship being a smart sailer, they were soon convinced that there was no chance of overhauling us.

"One night we had received orders from the captain that the whole watch should keep a sharp lookout for land ahead and just at daybreak the cry of 'land-ho' was heard from a man stationed on the foretop-sail yard. The captain and mate at once went up to the maintop-sail yard, where they remained nearly an hour, scanning the horizon in the direction where land had been re-ported. When they returned to the deck it was noticed that the captain's demeanor to the mate had taken a decided change for the better. Perhaps he had plainly told the latter what he intended to do, after which he no doubt thought it prudent to treat his subordinate with a little more respect, considering that he had taken the responsibility of making him an outlaw without his consent.

"At three o'clock or thereabouts, during the afternoon, a small boat was described by the lookout. It appeared to be about two or three miles distant and, as near as could be made out, her crew were pulling toward the ship. When this was reported to the captain, he directed the man at the wheel to steer for her. We soon overhauled the boat and found her full of Negroes, whom I afterward learned were kroomen.* These kroomen were black as coal tar and perfectly naked. They were sitting on the gunwales of their boat and propelling her with paddles. Standing up in the bow was a powerfully built Negro holding in his right hand a bright-red rag which he kept waving to and fro. The crew kept time with their paddles to the motion of this rag and at every stroke they gave utterance to curious sounds, which much resembled the noise made by a flock of crows. Right amidships of the boat we could see a white man, of dark complexion, who we afterward knew as 'the Spaniard.' He was straddling a cask and by his vehement gesticulation seemed to be urging the kroomen to do their best.

"The maintop-sail was now braced aback. As soon as the boat had reached us our friend of the cask mounted the ladder put over the side. Upon gaining the deck he rushed toward our skipper and threw his arms around his neck, shook his hand again and again and kept up such a constant fire of words that no opportunity was given the latter to open his mouth. The Spaniard finally recovered somewhat from the excitement of the meeting, after which the captain invited him into the cabin.

"As they went below orders were given to the kroomen to come on board and to make the boat fast astern, giving her plenty of scope by using a line from the ship. After this we were directed to 'fill away and stand in closer to the beach.' We ran toward land as far as was safe, when the ship was again hove-to. The boat's crew consisted of nineteen or twenty kroomen, all large and muscular fellows. They were all naked, not even having on a hat to protect their heads from the rays of a sun that would have melted the skulls of us white men, had we not had them well covered. Each one had a string of cowries tied round his ankles

* Members of the Kroo tribe of the Pepper Coast of Guinea, related to the Mandingoes.

and wrists. These I supposed, were used in lieu of money for bartering. Two or three of them could speak a little broken English. This they had probably learned from the sailors of the English men-of-war frequenting the coast.

"After a brief consultation our visitors selected one of their number to act as spokesman. He at once made good use of his knowledge of the English language by begging for something to eat. This we supplied. After their hunger was appeased they commenced begging, through their interpreter, for old shirts, hats, tobacco, and everything else they could see or think of. Some of our men went below and brought up a lot of old hats, shirts, etc., which they offered to exchange for the cowries worn by the Negroes on their ankles and wrists. The kroomen seemed loath to part with these at first, but the sight of a red flannel shirt was too tempting an object for the leader (the knight of the red rag in the boat) to resist and he soon succumbed. After this it was an easy thing to strike up a trade with them. For an old shirt I secured a small string of cowries, which are still in my possession. It was a ludicrous sight to behold them strutting up and down the deck in their new attire. None was completely· clad. One fellow had on a sou'wester and a short skirt; another, only a pair of overalls; and another, a pair of old seaboots and a straw hat. This last was the most extraordinary toilet I had ever seen.

"The captain and his Spanish friend now came on deck and on beholding the fantastic appearance of the kroomen, gave vent to a tremendous roar. The boat was hauled to the gangway and her funny looking crew ordered into her and after giving our skipper another affectionate embrace the Spaniard took his departure. The maintop-sail was once more filled away and we stood out to sea, braced up sharp on the wind.

"On the day following our departure from the coast the vessel was put under easy sail and the lookout again took up his quarters on the main top-gallant yard, with instructions to report every blow he saw. The captain was anxious to take every fish we could see that would yield any oil, no matter how small the quantity. I don't think the captain cared anything about the quality, however; it was the quantity he wanted, should we be boarded by the commander of a cruiser while on the coast.

"About this time our grub began to improve. The salt-horse kid was now accompanied with pickled onions, canned meats and other luxuries. Meanwhile 'Bungs,' the ship's cooper, was kept busy making small kids* and as fast as he finished a lot we spliced rope handles in them. Away down in the run, with many things piled on top of them, we had some time before brought to light about forty of the same suspicious-looking kids. Later on it will be seen the use they were put to.

"After our departure from the African coast we cruised about for a period of two weeks and during the time not a word was spoken by our captain which would even lead us to infer that the vessel was there for the purpose of carrying off a cargo of Negroes. Of course there could be no doubt of it — that we felt sure of; but what his reasons were for not imparting some information on the subject at this stage of affairs, was a mystery we could not solve. Even if the men had the will to remonstrate, they were powerless to do anything. There was not another person on board who had sufficient knowledge of navigation to take charge of the ship and he knew it. The mate of a merchantman is supposed to be a competent navigator, but in this instance the rule did not hold good. Our mate knew less of navigation than I did, for I could figure out a day's work by dead-reckoning and that was more than he could do.

"The whaling humbug was played out now. The reporting of 'blows' was still carried on, but no boats were ever after lowered for this purpose. During this whole two weeks I doubt if we were at any time more than ninety or a hundred miles distant from

* A kid is a small wooden tub.

the coast, for the distance run off was generally recovered at the end of every forty-eight hours, by sailing the other way.

"One night shortly after all the preparation had been done, the yards were squared and the course altered. The man at the wheel was cautioned to be very careful with his steering. The captain remained on deck all night. Sleep was out of the question in the forecastle and the watch below laid down on their seachests. At last the long dreary night came to an end, and as I expected, at the break of day the cry of 'land-ho' was heard from aloft. At that cry the captain exhibited openly his nervousness or cowardice. He directed the mate to go aloft with a spy-glass to look all around inshore and if he saw the least appearance of a vessel to report it immediately. The seamen were ordered on deck, to be prepared for anything.

"The part of the coast we were approaching appeared to be uninhabited, with a dense thicket two or three hundred yards back of the beach. As we came nearer I could see a long, low shed, just on the outskirts of the thicket facing the water. During all this time the captain had been nervously moving about and every five or ten minutes hailing the mate to inquire if he saw anything yet.

"After the mate had been aloft nearly three hours, he sighted a schooner at anchor off shore from the shed. A boat was put out and met the ship four or five hundred yards from the beach.

"Our friend, the 'palm oil trader,' stepped on board and gave our captain another affectionate kiss. He was very much excited and I inferred from his actions that he desired the ship brought at once to anchor. The captain seemed to think differently, for he continued to run her in and did not anchor until we were dangerously near the breakers. The sails were allowed to hang in the buntlines, not half hauled up, and even the royals did not have the turn of a gasket around them. It was surprising that the ship did not drag her anchor, with so much sail for the wind to act on. She lay hard aback and kept the small scope of chain out as taut as a harp-string.

" 'Let everything hang as it is,' sang the captain to the mate. 'And send all hands into the hold to put down the flooring. Don't be particular, but bear a hand.'

"We went below and commenced to execute this order. The 'palm oil merchant' danced up and down the deck like a lunatic and every minute or two poked his head down the main-hatch and ordered us to 'hurree uppe.' No such driving was necessary, however, for we had sense enough to realize that our anchor was down in a dangerous place and we worked with a will. We soon had the flooring laid; not very smoothly, it is true, but well enough to answer the purpose for the present.

" 'Man the boats, men. Step smart now, my lads,' was the next order.

"We tumbled into our boats and shoved clear of the ship. We had pulled but a short distance when a large surfboat passed us, crammed full of naked Negroes — men, women and children.

"She was manned by kroomen and they were using paddles to propel her. They were all jabbering at once in their lingo and every few minutes I could see a paddle raised and brought down on the head of some unlucky Negro.

"The boats stopped just outside the breakers and waited there while canoes manned by kroomen and loaded with Negroes were skillfully brought through the surf to them.

"We were nearly swamped by a number of them getting on one side of the boat as they piled into her. After they were all in we shipped the oars and started for our vessel, the surfboat returning to the beach for another load. We made slow progress, the boat being so overloaded that it was impossible to take a fair stroke without chafing the backs of the Negroes or striking them in the face with the oars.

"When we finally reached the ship they were passed up the

ladder until they came within the grips of two swarthy Portuguese stationed in the gangway. These men, who had come from the shore in the first boat, hauled the Negroes up on deck. The poor creatures were much scratched and bruised by this rough handling.

"After discharging our freight we started for another load, which we obtained in the same manner and we landed them safely on board. In this way we went back and forth until the last Negro was put aboard the ship, when the boats were hoisted. During this time we had been thus engaged, the large surfboats from the beach, although loaded to their utmost capacity with Negroes, had strange to say, made their way in every case through the breakers without losing a man.

"When we arrived on board everything was in confusion. The Negroes had been put into the hold without the least regard for stowage. Consequently, they were literally piled on one another; and the unsteady motion of the ship, combined with the foul air and great heat, made the place simply horrible. Naturally they were nearly all dreadfully sick at the stomach. The women had been put into the steerage. The ship had what sailors call a high poop-deck — that is, the cabin had been built on the maindeck. The forward part had been partitioned off and the staterooms removed as far as practicable, leaving almost a clear deck to the dividing line. This we called the steerage. The wind circulated freely through it; therefore, it could be called a Paradise compared with the hold. Hence, the women fared much better than the men.

"Now that our cargo was secured, the ship made sail and the remainder of the day was spent feeding and watering the cargo. Early the next morning preparations were made to get a meal ready for the Negroes. One of the try-pots was filled about three-quarters full of rice and two of the most intelligent of the blacks was appointed cooks, the cooper acting as superintendent. While this was being done we went down into the hold to see how they had fared during the dreadful night that had just passed. Their haggard looks bore evidence of the misery they had undergone. Pent up in such close quarters and inhaling such a terrible stench, it was miraculous that one-half of them had not perished. We found five or six dead bodies which were at once hoisted to the deck and consigned to the deep. There was no pretence of any religious ceremony. Just as they were, naked and forlorn, they were tossed overboard and for a long time we could see the bodies floating in the wake of the ship. I could not stay below long for the stench almost suffocated me. On reaching the deck I heard the captain say that at eight bells the Negroes must all be ordered up on deck to mess and while they were thus employed we should thoroughly cleanse the hold.

"Just before seven bells the captain notified the crew that there would be no more forenoon watches below, for we were so short-handed that no one could be spared from duty during the day. We were also told that, purely as a matter of safety, all hands ought to remain on deck in the daytime, lest the Negroes might feel their power when they saw how weak in numbers we were. We could say nothing against this arrangement, for it looked reasonable enough. We must be satisfied with eight hours' rest every other night, or perhaps even with less; for, should it be necessary to shorten sail, all hands would certainly be required on deck.

"The crew breakfasted at seven o'clock and at half-past seven we turned to and commenced operations by sending the Negroes on deck. After the deck was filled so completely that there was scarcely room enough to give us a chance to feed them, we found that a great number would have to remain below and mess there. They were now divided off into messes and the kids were filled by the cooper and his cooks with the rice, which they had all ready, and smoking hot, by this time. The kids were passed around to the messes and, in addition to the rice, each man was allowed two sea-biscuits. Very few of them had any inclination to eat, but the Spaniard, who took exclusive charge of them, seized a rope's end and raised their appetites by showering blows on their bare shoulders. The poor Negroes, being thus forcibly compelled to eat, quickly stuck their forefingers into the hot rice, and taking up some, put it into their mouths. It being very hot they rolled it about with their tongues and their eyes looked as if they would burst from their sockets before it was cool enough to swallow. After two or three meals they learned to cool it before putting it into their mouths.

"This feeding consumed nearly three hours; the hard usage they received, combined with the nausea caused by the sea-sickness, making it difficult for them to swallow or to retain any food on their stomachs. After the kids were removed, a tin pot, containing about a quart of fresh water, was passed to each one of them.

"Before proceeding farther it would, perhaps, be well to describe the Negroes. The kroomen were in every respect superior to the others. Large and well-built, with every appearance of robust health, they would undoubtedly bring the highest price in the market. They could all understand the Portuguese language and hence were invaluable to the Spaniards as interpreters. On the plantation where our cargo had been confined, prior to the time when they had been sent to the barracoon, the kroomen acted as bosses over the others. On board the ship they were armed with whips and given authority to abuse and beat the common Negroes whenever they felt like it. It seemed to me that they felt like it much oftener than was necessary and took an actual pleasure in doing it.

"These men did certain parts of the work and at night kept order and silence in the hold. The business of feeding the Negroes was entrusted to them. We merely superintended the operation and saw that each received the proper allowance and no more.

We never had occasion to punish them, as they faithfully performed the work allotted to them.

"The other Negroes numbered about eight hundred and included all sizes and ages — from infants at the breast to men and women of forty. Many of them were branded with curious devices. In some cases the whole body was covered with marks — not even the face being excepted. A large number also had the front teeth filed, like the kroomen, and when they opened their lips they looked hideous. They (the men) also were arrant cowards. The women were the pluckiest and had they all been of that sex we should probably have had a mutiny on board before the ship had been at sea two weeks. They numbered about two hundred and were stowed in the poop, as I said before. They were, with a few exceptions, all fine specimens of their race physically. Five or six of the younger ones were hopelessly sick — consumption it was, I believe, the complaint. They made more noise at night than all the males together. While on watch I often saw the Spaniard, whip in hand, bounce in among them and fiercely cut right and left. This treatment would have the desired effect, for that night at least.

"We had about fifty or sixty boys on board, ranging from six to fourteen years of age. They were all sound in body and enjoyed excellent health. The little fellows made no trouble at night, the awful looks of the kroomen acting like magic in suppressing any such tendency.

"Among the little girls the Spaniard was a great favorite and I cannot recall a single time when he punished them or caused it to be done by the kroomen. During many a hot, sultry day, when the awning was spread across the maindeck, he would permit the little ones to gambol and play under it, often exerting his fancy to assist their childish amusements. He would frequently take small strips of calico, eighteen or twenty inches in length, tie them in the rigging, and then start a race, giving each an equal

chance, to see who could secure one of the pieces. This was a
prize to the lucky one, and she was regarded with envy by those
who failed to secure a strip. The calico was afterward put to a
practical use in the way of aprons. The Spaniard was also well
skilled in medicine and by his intelligent treatment of the sick
saved a number of lives.

"As soon as the Negroes were sent below after their first meal,
he arranged for feeding them in the future at regular intervals.
At eight o'clock in the morning breakfast was to be served. Then
the kids were to be rinsed out, filled with salt-water and one
passed to each mess, the members of which should be made to
wash their hands and faces. After this, every man, woman and
child was to be allowed one quart of water each. The same pro-
gram was to be enforced at the afternoon meal, which was to
commence at three o'clock. At first it required nearly three hours
for each meal, but after a week's practice, the time was reduced
to about two hours.

"On the first day, when we had finished feeding them in the
afternoon, it was six o'clock, the time appointed for all the Negroes to be stowed away for the night. After the deck was
cleared we went below to see that the kroomen arranged them
properly. Commencing forward, we made the first man lie down,
head to windward, facing toward the bow, and the knees slightly
drawn toward the chin. Another one was then placed alongside,
with his breast touching the back of the first and his knees bent
at a similar angle. In this manner we stowed them, in tiers, the
length and width of the hold. The kroomen were allowed the
privilege of reclining as they chose, but it was their duty to keep
the others in their proper places. When daylight came the Negroes
could change their position to suit themselves.

"At five o'clock every morning we commenced to wash down
the maindeck, which was also the signal for the cooper to call
his cooks and prepare the food for the Negroes. After scrubbing

and scraping until seven o'clock the watch on deck would call the watch below and all hands go to breakfast. We were allowed half an hour for breakfast, after which the Negroes had to be sent on deck and arranged in their proper messes for the meal. In the course of a week's time we had them nicely regulated, and after that there was no further trouble.

"A number of sick Negroes were found below and a makeshift hospital was made under a tarpaulin on deck. All the invalids were conveyed there and received prompt treatment. Dysentery, caused largely no doubt by the change of diet and water, was the principal and most fatal disease that attacked them. After lingering a long time, and suffering greatly, the first patients all died. Two or three cases of smallpox broke out, which received prompt treatment, but these also were fatal. It was providential that this loathesome disease did not spread. Had it done so, God only knows what would have been our fate. There occurred one remarkable case which the captain called the coast scurvy. The man sick with it swelled until his skin was transparent. No medicine gave him relief of any kind and his sufferings were terrible to witness. He lived fully two weeks in dreadful agony before death relieved him. There was a case of palsy among the males and the Spanish captain could do nothing for it. When the poor victim took the watercup in his hand it would shake very much and this pleased the Negroes so that they would shout and laugh at an immoderate rate. Sometimes an application of the whip was necessary to quiet them.

"Only one birth occurred in the passage. A woman was delivered of twins — one dead and the other living but a few hours after birth.

"When the Negroes were all below and stowed for the night, one of the watch was stationed at each hatch to guard it for two hours. At the expiration of this time he was relieved by another and so on until daylight. While on this duty the men were armed with native African swords or knives which the Spanish captain supplied. They looked like rusty cheese-knives and, in my opinion, the only thing they were good for was to bang against the combings of the hatch. When the Negroes were noisy the watch would yell out something which sounded like 'Yock Ho.' This always acted like magic for on hearing it they would quiet down instantly.

"The crew expressed a wish for revolvers to protect themselves in case of a sudden attack in force, but the Spanish captain said the sight of these rusty old knives would have inspired more fear than a dozen revolvers, the bulk of the Negroes not even knowing the use of a pistol and hence having no fear of it. I thought that story would do 'to tell to the marines.' The crew, fully armed with revolvers, would have been a formidable force and in case of a misunderstanding with the afterguards, would have held the balance of power.

"The hatches also were left open day and night and on occasions several of the Negroes below would disregard the orders of the kroomen and come to the hatchway. A slap over the head with the flat side of the sword, given by the man on watch, was something they could better understand and it never failed to be followed by an instant disappearance on the part of the offendor.

"One morning a krooman reported to the Spanish captain a Negro who had resisted his authority during the night. The offendor was hustled on deck, stretched out at full length, face downward and tied to the ring-bolts. One of the kroomen now commenced to lash the poor creature over the back and when he flagged another took his place and renewed the beating. The Negro was grit to the bone and made not the slightest outcry. Not until life was almost extinct did the Spaniard order him released. It was the latter's wish to draw blood, but the Negro's hide was so tough it could not be done by thrashing.

"For several weeks after leaving the African Coast, in consequence of light winds and calms, the vessel made a poor run, so that there was every prospect of a long voyage. About this time the allowance of water was reduced. There was no change made in the allowance of food, for we had an ample stock on board. On the contrary, the Negroes were fed better, a certain quantity of pork and beef being given them twice a week. Good care and plenty to eat made a marked improvement in their appearance, at which the Spanish captain was proportionately pleased. A fine healthy Negro would bring a much higher price than a puny, sickly one; therefore to feed them well and take good care of them meant an increase of doubloons to the owners. Up to this period we had lost but about twenty and this mortality was caused principally by dysentery. When the wind was light during the day the maindeck awning was spread and the Negroes in the hold were allowed to come up and stretch their limbs. This was a great relief from the intense heat and foul air of the hold and was no doubt the cause of saving a number of lives.

"The water casks were refilled during a shower one day and the shortage was eased considerably. About this time the captain's drunkenness got out of hand. The ship had five or six barrels of New England rum and the crew occasionally sneaked drinks, sucking it out through a straw. Then the captain appropriated it all to himself and by 4 P.M. every day was dead drunk. He would then retire to a spare boat on the poop-deck and sleep off the effects. The Spanish captain remonstrated him and pointed out the bad example he was setting the crew. Argument had no effect, however, for he continued to drink until the cargo was disposed of.

"One afternoon an occurrence took place which came near resulting seriously. Just before arriving at the sleep-drunk stage he always manifested a very ugly temper and usually relieved himself by cursing the men. During the earlier part of the afternoon mentioned the wind had died out and the ship was becalmed. The yards were squared and the courses hauled up to prevent chafing. The captain came on deck and gave orders to set the studding sails. This was useless, as there was no wind and the officers told him so. He then began to swear at the officer of the deck and told him to go below, after which he bawled out to the men to reeve the gear. Having had plenty of work all the forenoon and scarcely any rest during the previous night, they were not in the humor for such unnecessary labor and, as they took the gear in hand to reeve, there was much audible growling. The captain had just rum enough in him to forget the kind of voyage the ship was on and he cursed and threatened to trice up the first man he heard growl.

"This was too much to take from him and the men threw the gear on deck and made a move toward him. Very opportunely for the old man the Spanish captain came on deck and took in the situation at a glance. Placing himself between the ladder that led to the poop and the men, he vehemently gesticulated and said, 'No, no. Bad — very bad.' He called the officers and told them to tell the men not to do anything rash, for the captain was drunk and did not know what he was doing. It was some time before the men could be pacified and induced to go forward. I think the captain must have been sensible of his danger, for, drunk as he was, he had the prudence to go below instead of lying down in the boat as he had done on former occasions. This was a good lesson for him. He never again threatened to trice us up and his orders were not embellished with so many disgusting oaths as heretofore.

"About this time the Negroes were given their first bath. They were hustled upon deck and arranged in tiers, standing. The hose was now attached to the head-pump and a lively stream squirted over them. They laughed and chattered good-naturedly while receiving this ducking. After being confined in the hold all night the cool sea-water must have been very refreshing.

"The voyage went smoothly for the most part. A sail was seen but the ship was able to avoid it. On Monday afternoons, the crew fumigated the hold with smoke from burning tar. At one point, one of the Negroes was discovered stealing water by unbunging a water cask, inserting a long stick and then drawing it quick enough to catch the water droplets in his hand. Several were involved but only the one who withdrew the bung was discovered. The Spaniard had him brought on deck and lashed to the ringbolts where the kroomen beat him unmercifully.

"The punishment continued so long that I thought the man would have died under it, but his endurance was wonderful and he only uttered a few groans. When the beating was finally discontinued the Spaniard stooped down alongside of him and taking a razor out of his pocket, opened it and cut long, straight gashes in the flesh. Afterward he took a flat piece of wood, resembling a ruler and beat gently all around the wounds which had the effect of making them bleed freely. Having accomplished this he ordered his Negro assistant to get a pot full of brine out of the harness cask and apply it to the bleeding wounds. When this was done the poor Negro could suppress his anguish no longer and groaned aloud. After being kept in this awful agony for ten minutes he was released from the ringbolts and put in double irons.

"The captain of the ship and all the crew witnessed this inhuman punishment and I will give our own commander credit for having more heart than the Spaniard for he told him he was too severe on the Negro. The crew were all bitterly incensed against the 'd —— Dago,' as they called him and gave vent to their feelings by calling him a 'bloody cannibal' and expressing a desire to serve him the same way to see how he would like it.

"This was the only Negro punished in this manner. I think if it had been attempted again the captain would have interfered and if he had not the men would have prevented it. The unfortunate victim of the Spaniard's cruelty did not recover while on board and was still very sick when landed.

"When the Negroes were again watered we received orders to give them a full allowance — about a quart. Perhaps the captains were afraid thirst would make them desperate at night and thought it would be better to allow them a little more water than to have them steal it.

"One day as we drew close to the Indies, the carpenter and I were ordered to scrape off the ship's name from the stern. We were now outlaws and would be a prize for any vessel strong enough to capture us. The ship might be taken but the captain swore that the Negroes never should. In case of such an emergency, he would 'walk them all overboard and send them to hell.'

"The voyage, however, was soon to be ended, for the fine winds we had experienced during the past two weeks had brought us near the island of Cuba. Every thread of canvas that the ship could carry had been spread, which made her jump through the water like a racehorse. My whole thoughts were centered on this breeze and if it moderated a little, down went my spirits; but if it increased, up they would go.

"A day or so before the ship reached the shipping lanes through the Indies, the crew painted the ship black and a narrow yellow ribbon running around the hull. From the appearance of a whaler, the vessel was transformed more to the appearance of a merchantman, more likely to appear in those waters. The whale boats were hove overboard, as were a large number of harpoons and lances and other whaling gear.

"On a Monday afternoon land was sighted and shortly afterwards the sail of a small sloop. Both of the captains watched her movements intently. The strong breeze soon brought her close to us, when our fore-royal halyards were let go. As the yard settled down it was answered by the slacking down of her peak. This seemed to dispel all doubt in the minds of the two captains and the ship was hove to immediately. The peak of the sloop's mainsail was hoisted when she came within hailing distance and luffed up in the wind. The Spanish captain now hailed her in his own language and after a short conversation with the sloop's skipper we were ordered to man the starboard boat. This was done and we lowered her and pulled alongside of the sloop. Her skipper jumped in and we brought him to the ship. He remained some time in conversation with our captain, the Spaniard in the meantime writing a letter. This he gave to his visitor, together with some verbal instructions, after which we carried the latter back to his sloop. As soon as we had shoved clear of his vessel's side he at once made sail and stood in for the land.

"After the boat was hoisted we filled away the main-topsail and stood off shore. This disappointed all hands for we expected that the Negroes were to be landed and to now see her head turned seaward was a great disappointment. It afterward transpired that the skipper of the sloop had been on the lookout for us for some time to deliver instructions. We also learned that arrangements had to be made to send out a couple of small craft to receive our cargo. These vessels were to lay outside of the cruising ground of the men-of-war that patrolled this part of the coast. We were to lay off shore, as much out of danger as possible, until Saturday morning, by which time we must come back to the position we had left.

"The designated time arrived and the seamen and cargo alike became tense. The Negroes became very much excited and made a great deal of noise and all the threats of the Spaniard had no effect in quieting them. Had any vessel passed near us I think the people on board would have been astonished at hearing such a bedlam of sounds. Two or three lights were reported by the men on lookout but we easily avoided them.

"The night finally came to an end as even the longest one must. We then swallowed a hasty breakfast, after which a stage was rigged to put over the side. This was afterward used in transferring the Negroes. During all this time the lookouts had continued their vigilance but no sign of any small vessels could be seen on any part of the horizon. At four bells (ten o'clock) land was made out from the fore top-gallant yard. The captain now considered the ship close enough in and had her hove-to.

"A little before twelve o'clock a sail was reported inshore and to the westward of our ship and a few minutes later another one was made out in about the same position. The captain now took the spyglass and went aloft where he remained fully an hour watching the strangers. During the time we made out the two vessels to be schooners. By two o'clock they were near enough to signal, when the fore-royal yard was settled down and a few minutes later we hauled down the flying jib. Every eye was now intently watching them and if our signals should not be answered, adieu to our hopes for today. After being kept in suspense for ten or fifteen minutes the welcome answer was made. It was received with three rousing cheers which fairly made the old ship tremble.

"The schooners drew close to the ship and were secured alongside. The captain sung out 'Five or six men stand by the lines and the rest get the stage over the side.'

"This was promptly done and ladders were also put down the hatchways for the Negroes to mount when the order should be given.

"There was some trouble in making the schooners fast but the word finally came for several men to go below and start the Negroes up the ladders. Others were stationed in the waist to assist them over to the stage between the vessels. During that time, a large valise was now passed from one of the schooners to the ship and was taken charge of by the captain. We later learned it was filled with doubloons.

"As fast as the Negroes reached the deck they were given a crack with the whip to make them move quickly and then shoved over the side on the stage, from which they had to jump to the schooner's deck. It took an hour to clear out the hold and then came the women's turn. I thought it would be difficult to make them jump from the stage, but they did not seem to mind and succeeded very well.

"The kroomen were the last to leave and as they passed over they were given tobacco and old clothes. Every Negro being reported out of the ship, the order was given to cast off the lines and fill-away.

"While we had been engaged unloading the Negroes, the other schooner had hauled alongside her mate and had taken on board about one-half of them. Both vessels were filled with Negroes and the problem how to prevent their wooly heads from being seen by a passing vessel, should one get near enough, I left for the Spaniard to solve.

"Just as we braced up, the Spaniard sung out from the schooner's deck for us to send him some hardtack. The captain ordered four barrels thrown overboard, taking an oath that he wouldn't lower a boat for the devil himself.

"Sail was made on the schooners and their bows pointed toward the land. We also put every rag of canvas that would draw on our ship. Our progress was slow, however, the wind being hardly strong enough to keep the sails full. The captain gave orders to throw the kids overboard and after this job was done he wanted the pine flooring in the hold taken up and piled aft. The mate said it was getting too dark below to work and it had better be left until morning. This was decided on and I went forward to the top-gallant forecastle and watched the receding schooners until the shadows of night enveloped them.

"The ship was then run to Campeachy, Yucatan, and anchored on the banks off that port. Prior to this we had thrown overboard all the pine flooring that had been used during the passage from Africa, after which chloride of lime was generously sprinkled throughout the hold. No amount of this disinfectant had the effect of totally eradicating the peculiar odor that infected the hold and we finally decided that nothing but fire could purify it perfectly.

"The crew would no longer remain by the ship, although the captain was urgent for them to do so, but went on shore and secured board in the city of Campeachy. They behaved as most sailors do when they have any cash in their pockets and as they had been liberally paid in Spanish doubloons, they fairly 'took the roof off the town.'

"After being in Campeachy about three weeks we embarked in a Mexican schooner for New Orleans, where we arrived in January 1861. The most intense excitement prevailed in New Orleans at the time and I had doubts of being able to get north, should my departure be delayed. I therefore came at once by rail to New York. Shortly after I made a voyage to China and on my return to America I entered the navy as a volunteer officer where I remained until after the close of the rebellion."

Manning thus ended his adventure on the slaving voyage of the *Thomas Watson*. The *Thomas Watson* later was reported to have been the first American ship in England to fly Confederate colors. In October 1861, while attempting to run the Union blockade at Charleston, South Carolina, she ran aground while being pursued by blockading Federal cruisers. Her cargo that time was salt, blankets and flannels earmarked for Southern armies. While stranded on the reef outside of Charleston, the *Thomas Watson* burned to the water's edge on October 15, 1861.

10

SLAVE MUTINY

As HAS BEEN INDICATED EARLIER, slave mutinies aboard ship were one of the greatest fears of mariners in the slave trade. Captains and crew knew full well they could expect no mercy from the slaves once the latter were in control of the ship. For this reason, the slightest move toward revolt brought harsh punishment for any offender.

Most of the uprisings occurred just before the slave ships left the Guinea Coast, or shortly thereafter, when the slaves were still fresh and in good physical shape. Their strength and spirits were drained fast during the confinement of the holds in the middle passage. Revolt was encouraged by the fact that many slaves believed that when they died they immediately returned to their homelands, and thus a last ditch effort to escape, even at the cost of their lives, was feared less than the prospect of continuing the voyage.

That ship captains often employed the most brutal methods to curb a shipboard insurrection, is illustrated in the following account contained in the official report of the U.S. Consul in Liberia in the 1850's to the secretary of state about an insurrection aboard the *Kentucky*, an American slave ship.* The insurrec-

* John R. Spears, *The American Slave Trade*. London, 1900.

tion had been speedily put down, but the *Kentucky*'s captain, fearing a recurrence, was determined to give the leaders a lesson.

"They were ironed, or chained, two together, and when they were hung, a rope was put around their necks and they were drawn up to the yardarm clear of the sail. This did not kill them, but only choked or strangled them. They were then shot in the breast and the bodies were thrown overboard. If only one of the two that were ironed together was to be hung, the rope was put around his neck and he was drawn up clear of the deck and his leg laid across the rail and chopped off to save the irons and release him from his companion, who at the same time lifted up his leg until the other was chopped off, as aforesaid, and he released. The bleeding Negro was then drawn up, shot in the breast and thrown overboard. The legs of about one dozen were chopped off this way. When the feet fell on the deck, they were picked up by the crew and thrown overboard, and sometimes they shot at the body while it still hung, living, and all sorts of sport was made of the business."

Henry Harrison, a sailor aboard a Liverpool slave ship, tells of his ship's capture by slaves off Mana. The captain had purchased more than one hundred slaves who mutinied, killing nearly all of the crew. Harrison, one of the few survivors, wrote his relatives of the slaughter in a letter from the Plantains on the Guinea Coast on April 23, 1759.*

"On the 12th of January, we had the misfortune to be cut off by the Negroes. They killed Captain Potter, our surgeon, carpenter, cooper and James Steward, a boy. Luckily the captain had sent me on shore that morning to the King's town, about ten miles up the river, to fetch slaves down; but before I reached the town, we met two of his servants bringing a slave down. We returned with them, made a smoke on the shore as a signal for our boat, but before we had it made well, saw her put off from the

* Williams, *Liverpool Privateers*. London, 1897.

vessel with six of our people, being all left alive on board. I swam
off to her and we rowed for the *Spencer*, Capt. Daniel Cooke, then
lying at Cape Mount. At one o'clock that night, Captain Cooke
got under way, and made sail in order to attempt to recover our
vessel; at daylight, finding her at anchor, he fired his guns into her
for about an hour, but I could not persuade him to board her.
That evening the slaves ran the snow on shore. We had purchased 103 slaves, and had a pledge for two more on board. . . .
When this fatal accident happened, our chief mate was gone with
the yawl to windward, and the boatswain with the long boat to
leeward to purchase slaves. Mr. Eaton and the boatswain got on
board Captain Nichols, and I heard that they saved 15 or 16
slaves that were due to us on shore, and left Mana, Mar. 30,
designed for the West Indies."

There were many instances of such slave mutinies in the history of the trade. One veteran slave ship captain, William Snelgrave, wrote in the 1730's of how he prevented slave insurrections and how those he had seen could have been avoided.* His
methods, though not universal, were at least those of an experienced slave ship commander.

"These mutinies are generally occasioned by the sailors' ill
usage of these poor people, when on board the ships wherein
they are transported to our plantations. Wherever, therefore, I
have commanded, it has been principal care to have the Negroes
on board my ship kindly used; and I have always strictly charged
my white people to treat them with humanity and tenderness. In
which I have usually found my account, both in keeping them
from mutinying and preserving them in health."

"And whereas it may seem strange to those that are unacquainted with the method of managing them, how we can carry
so many hundreds together in a small ship, and keep them in

* William Snelgrave, *A New Account of Some Parts of Guinea and the Slave
Trade*. London, 1734.

order, I shall just mention what is generally practised. When we purchase grown people, I acquaint them by the interpreter, 'That, now they are become my property, I think fit to let them know what they are bought for, that they may be easy in their minds.' " In parentheses, Snelgrave added: "For these poor people are generally under terrible apprehensions upon their being bought by white men, many being afraid that we design to eat them, which I have been told, is a story much credited by the inland Negroes."

"So, after informing them, that they are bought to till the ground in our country, with several other matters, I then acquaint them how they are to behave themselves on board toward the white men, that if any one abuses them, they are to complain to the linguist, who is to inform me of it, and I will do them justice. But if they make a disturbance, or offer to strike a white man, they must expect to be severely punished.

"When we purchase the Negroes, we couple the sturdy men together with irons, but we suffer the women and children to go freely about. And soon after we have sail'd from the coast, we undo all of the men's irons.

"They are fed twice a day, and are allowed in fair weather to come on deck at seven o'clock in the morning, and to remain there, if they think proper, till sun setting. Every Monday morning they are served with pipes and tobacco, which they are very fond of. The men Negroes lodge separate from the women and children, and the places where they all lye are cleaned every day, some white men being appointed to see them do it.

"The first mutiny I saw among the Negroes happened during my first voyage, in the year 1704. It was on board the *Eagle Galley* of London, commanded by my father, with whom I was as purser. We had bought our Negroes in the river of Old Callabar in the Bay of Guinea. At the time of their mutinying, we were in that river, having four hundred of them on board, and not above ten white men who were able to do service. For several of our ship's company were dead and many more sick. Besides, two of our boats were just then gone with twelve people on shore to fetch wood, which lay in sight of the ship. All these circumstances put the Negroes on consulting how to mutiny, which they did at four o'clock in the afternoon, just as they went to supper. But as we had always carefully examined the men's irons, both morning and evening, none had got them off, which in great measure contributed to our preservation. Three white men stood on the watch with cutlaces in their hands. One of them who was on the forecastle, a stout fellow, seeing some of the men Negroes take hold of the chief mate, in order to throw him overboard, he laid on them so heartily with the flat side of his cutlace that they soon quitted the mate, who escaped from them and ran on the quarter deck to get arms. I was then sick with an ague and lying on a couch in the great cabbin, the fit being just come on. However, I no sooner heard the outcry that the slaves were mutinying but I took two pistols and run on the deck with them, where, meeting with my father and the chief mate, I delivered a pistol to each of them. Whereupon they went forward on the booms, calling to the Negro men that were on the forecastle. But they did not regard their threats, being busy with the centry (who had disengaged the chief mate), and they would certainly have killed him with his own cutlace, could they have got it from him, but they could not break the line wherewith the handle was fastened to his wrist. And so, tho' they had seized him, yet they could not make use of his cutlace. Being thus disappointed, they endevoured to throw him overboard, but he held so fast by one of them that they could not do it. My father, seeing this stout man in so much danger, ventured amongst the Negroes, to save him, and fired his pistol over their heads, thinking to frighten them. But a lusty slave struck him with a billet so hard that he was almost stunned. The slave was going to repeat the blow, when a young lad about seventeen years old, whom we had been kind to, interposed his arm and received the blow, by which his arm-bone was fractured. At the same instant, the mate fired his pistol and shot the Negro that had struck my father. At the sight of this the mutiny ceased, and all the men Negroes on the forecastle threw themselves flat on their faces, crying out for mercy.

"Upon examining into the matter, we found, there were not above twenty men slaves concerned in this mutiny, and the two ringleaders were missing, having jumped overboard as soon as they found their project defeated, and were drowned. This was all the loss we suffered on this occasion. For the Negro that was shot by the mate, the surgeon, beyond all expectation, cured. And I had the good fortune to lose my ague by the fright and hurry I was put into. Moreover, the young man who had received the blow on his arm to save my father was cured by the surgeon in our passage to Virginia. At our arrival in that place we gave him his freedom, and a worthy gentleman, one Colonel Carter, took him into his service till he became well enough acquainted in the country to provide for himself.

"I have been several voyages when there has been no attempt made by our Negroes to mutiny, which I believe was owing chiefly to their being kindly used, and to my officers' care in keeping a good watch. But sometimes we meet with stout stubborn people amongst them, who are never to be made easy, and these are generally some of the Cormantines, a nation of the Gold Coast. I went in the year 1721, in the *Henry* of London, [on] a voyage to that part of the coast and bought a good many of these people. We were obliged to secure them very well in irons, and watch them narrowly. Yet they nevertheless mutinied, tho' they had little prospect of succeeding. I lay at that time near a place called Mumfort, on the Gold Coast, having near five hundred Negroes on board, three hundred of which were men. Our ship's company consisted of fifty white people, all in health, and I had very good officers, so that I was very easy in all respects.

"This mutiny began at midnight (the Moon then shining very bright) in this manner. Two men that stood centry at the fore-hatchway, where the men slaves came up to go to the house of office, permitted four to go to that place, but neglected to lay the gratings again, as they should have done. Whereupon four more Negroes came on deck, who had got their irons off, and the four in the house of office having done the same, all the eight fell on the two centries, who immediately called out for help. The Negroes endeavoured to get their cutlaces from them, but the lineyards (that is the lines by which the handles of the cutlaces were fastened to the men's wrists) were so twisted in the scuffle that they could not get them off before we came to their assistance. The Negroes, perceiving several white men coming toward them, with arms in their hands, quitted the centries and jumped over the ship's side into the sea.

"I being by this time come forward on the deck, my first care was to secure the gratings to prevent any more Negroes from coming up. And then I ordered people to get into the boat and save those that had jumped overboard, which they luckily did, for they found them all clinging to the cables the ship was moored by.

"After we had secured these people, I called the linguists and ordered them to bid the men Negroes between decks to be quiet (for there was a great noise among them). On their being silent, I asked, 'What had induced them to mutiny?' They answered, 'I was a great rogue to buy them, in order to carry them away from their own country, and that they were resolved to regain their liberty if possible.' I replied, 'That they had forfeited their freedom before I bought them, either by crimes, or by being taken in war, according to the custom of their country, and they being now my property, I was resolved to let them feel my resentment, if they abused my kindness. Asking at the same time, whether they had been ill used by the white men, or had wanted for anything the ship afforded. To this they replied, 'They had nothing to complain of.' Then I observed to them, 'That if they should gain their point and escape to the shore, it would be no advantage to them, because their countrymen would catch them, and sell them to other ships.'

"This served my purpose, and they seemed to be convinced of their fault, begging 'I would forgive them and promising for the future to be obedient, and never mutiny again, if I would not punish them this time.' This I readily granted, and so they went to sleep. When daylight came we called the men Negroes up on deck, and examining their irons, found them all secure. So this affair ended happily, which I was very glad of, for these people are the stoutest and most sensible Negroes on the coast. Neither are they so weak as to imagine as others do, that we buy them to eat them, being satisfied we carry them to work in our plantations, as they do in their own country.

"However, a few days after this, we discovered they were plotting again, and preparing to mutiny. Some of the ringleaders proposed to one of our linguists if he could procure them an ax, they would cut the cables the ship rid by in the night, and so on her driving (as they imagined) ashore, they should get out of our hands and then would become his [the linguist] servants as long as they lived.

"For the better understanding of this I must observe here that these linguists are natives and freemen of the country whom we hire on account of their speaking good English, during the time we remain trading on the coast, and they are likewise brokers between us and the black merchants.

"This linguist was so honest as to acquaint me with what had been proposed to him, and advised me to keep a strict watch over the slaves. For tho' he had represented to them the same as I had done on their mutinying before, that they would all be catch'd again, and sold to other ships in case they could carry their point and get on shore, yet it had no effect upon them.

"This gave me a good deal of uneasiness. For I knew several voyages had proved unsuccessful by mutinies, as they occasioned either the total loss of the ship and the white men's lives, or at least by rendering it absolutely necessary to kill or wound a great number of slaves in order to prevent a total destruction. Moreover, I knew many of these Cormantine Negroes despised punishment, and even death itself. It has often happened at Barbadoes and other islands, that on their being anyways hardly dealt with, to break them of their stubbornness in refusing to work, twenty or more have hang'd themselves at a time in a plantation.

"However, about a month after this a sad accident happened, that brought our slaves to be more orderly and put them in a better temper. And it was this. On our going from Mumfort to Annamaboe, which is the principal port on the Gold Coast, I met there with another of my owner's ships, called the *Elizabeth*. Captain Thompson, that commanded her, was dead, as also his chief mate. Moreover, the ship had afterwards been taken . . . on the windward coast by Roberts the Pirate, with whom several of the sailors belonging to her had entered. However, some of the pirates had hindered the cargo's being plundered and obtained that the ship should be restored to the second mate, telling him, 'They did it out of respect to the generous character his owner bore, in doing good to poor sailors.'

"When I met with this vessel I had almost disposed of my ship's cargo and the *Elizabeth* being under my direction, I acquainted the second mate, who then commanded her, that I thought it for our owner's interest, to take the slaves from on board him, being about 120, into my ship and then go off the coast. And that I would deliver him at the same time the remains of my cargo for him to dispose of with his own after I was sailed. This he readily complied with, but told me he feared his ship's company would mutiny and oppose my taking the slaves from him. And indeed, they came at that instant in a body on the quarterdeck, where one spoke for the rest, telling me plainly that they would not allow the slaves to be taken out by me. I found by this they had lost all respect for their present commander, who indeed was a weak man. However, I calmly asked the reason why they offered to oppose my taking the slaves. To which they answered, 'I had no business with them.' On this I desired the captain to send . . . for the book of instructions Captain Thompson had received from the owner, and he read to them, at my request, that part in which their former captain or his successor (in case of death) was to follow my orders. Hereupon they all cried out 'They should remain a great while longer on the coast to purchase more slaves if I took these from them, which they were resolved to oppose.' I answered 'That such of the ship's company as desired it, I would receive on board my own, where they should have the same wages they had at present on board the *Elizabeth*, and I would send some of my own people to supply their places.'

"This so reasonable an offer was refused, one of the men who was the ship's cooper telling me, that the slaves had been on board a long time and they had great friendship with them; therefore they would keep them. I asked him 'Whether he had ever been on the Coast of Guinea before? He replied no.' Then I told him 'I supposed he had not by his way of talking, and advised him not to rely on the friendship of slaves, which he might have reason to repent of when too late.' And 'tis remarkable this very person was killed by them the next night, as shall be presently related.

"So finding that reasoning with these men was to no purpose. I told them when I came with my boats to fetch the slaves, they should find me as resolute to chastise such of them as should dare

to oppose me, as I had been condescending to convince them by
arguing calmly. So I took my leave of their captain, telling him
I would come next morning to finish the affair.

"But that very night, which was near a month after the mutiny on board us at Mumfort, the moon shining now very bright
as it did then, we heard about ten o'clock two or three musquets
fired on board the *Elizabeth*. Upon that I ordered all our boats
to be manned, and having secured everything in our ship to prevent our slaves from mutinying, I went myself in our pinnace (the
other boats following me), on board the *Elizabeth*. In our way
we saw two Negroes swimming from her, but before we could
reach them with our boats, some sharks rose from the bottom
and tore them in pieces. We came presently along the side of the
ship where we found two men Negroes holding by a rope, with
their heads just above water. They were afraid it seems to swim
from the ship's side, having seen their companions devoured just
before by the sharks. These two slaves we took into our boat, and
then went into the ship, where we found the Negroes very quiet,
and all under deck. But the ship's company was on the quarter-
deck in a great confusion, saying 'The cooper, who had been
placed centry at the forehatchway, over the men Negroes, was,
they believed, killed by them.' I was surprized to hear this, won-
dering that these cowardly fellows who had so vigorously opposed
my taking the slaves out a few hours before, had not courage
enough to venture forward to save their shipmate, but had secured themselves by shutting the quarter-deck door, where they
all stood with arms in their hands.

"So I went to the forepart of the ship with some of my people, and there we found the cooper lying on his back, quite dead,
his scull being cleft asunder with a hatchet that lay by him. At the
sight of this I called for the linguist and bid him ask the Negroes
between decks, 'Who had kill'd the white man?' They answered
'They knew nothing of the matter, for there had been no design

of mutinying amongst them.' Which upon examination we found true; for above one hundred of the Negroes then on board, being brought to Windward, did not understand a word of the Gold Coast language, and so had not been in the plot. But this mutiny was contrived by a few Cormantee Negroes, who had been purchased about two or three days before. At last, one of the two men Negroes we had taken up along the ship side impeached his companion and he readily confessed he had kill'd the cooper, with no other view but that he and his countrymen might escape undiscovered by swimming on shore. For on their coming upon deck, they observed that all the white men set to watch were asleep, and having found the cook's hatchet by the fire-place, he took it up, not designing then to do any mischief with it, but passing by the cooper, who was centry and beginning to awake, the Negro rashly struck him on the head with it and then jumped overboard.

"Upon this frank confession, the white men would have cut him to pieces, but I prevented it, and carried him to my own ship. Early the next morning, I went on board the *Elizabeth* with my boats and sent away all the Negroes then in her into my own ship. Not one of the other ship's company offered to oppose it. Two of them, the carpenter and the steward, desired to go with me, which I readily granted, and by way of security for the future success of the voyage, I put my chief mate and four of my under officers (with their own consent) on board the *Elizabeth*. They arrived about five months after this at Jamaica, having disposed of most of the cargo.

"After having sent the slaves out of the *Elizabeth*, as I have just now mentioned, I went on board my own ship, and there being then in the road of Anamaboe, eight sail of ships besides us, I sent an officer in my boat to the commanders of them, 'To desire their company on board my ship, because I had an affair of great consequence to communicate to them.' Soon after, most of them were pleased to come, and I having acquainted them with the whole matter, and they having also heard the Negro's confession, 'That he had killed the white man,' they unanimously advised me to put him to death arguing 'That blood required blood, by all laws both divine and human, especially as there was in this case the clearest proof, namely the murderer's confession. Moreover this would in all probability prevent future mischiefs. For by publicly executing this person at the ship's foreyard arm, the Negroes on board their ships would see it and as they were very much disposed to mutiny, it might prevent them from attempting it.' These reasons, with my being in the same circumstances, made me comply.

"Accordingly we acquainted the Negro that he was to die in an hour's time for murdering the white man. He answered, 'He must confess it was a rash action in him to kill him, but he desired me to consider that if I put him to death, I should lose all the money I had paid for him.' To this I bid the interpreter reply, 'That tho' I knew it was customary in his country to commute for murder for a sum of money, yet it was not so with us, and he should find that I had no regard to my profit in this respect. For as soon as an hour-glass just turned was run out, he should be put to death.' At which I observed he showed no concern.

"Hereupon the other commanders went on board their respective ships, in order to have all their Negroes upon deck at the time of execution, and to inform them of the occasion of it. The hour-glass being run out, the murderer was carried on the ship's forecastle, where he had rope fastened under his arms, in order to be hoisted up to the foreyard arm, to be shot to death. This some of his countrymen observing, told him (as the linguist informed me afterwards), 'That they would not have him be frightened, for it was plain I did not design to put him to death, otherwise the rope would have been put about his neck to hang him.' For it seems they had no thought of his being shot, judging he was only to be hoisted up to the yardarm in order to scare him. But they immediately saw the contrary, for as soon as he was hoisted up, ten white men who were placed behind the barricado in the quarter-deck, fired their musquets and instantly killed him. This struck a sudden damp upon our Negro men, who thought that on account of my profit, I would not have executed him.

"The body being let down upon the deck, the head was cut off and thrown overboard. This last part was done to let our Negroes see that all who offended thus should be served in the same manner. For many of the blacks believe that if they are put to death and not dismembered, they shall return again to their own country, after they are thrown overboard. But neither the person that was executed, nor his countrymen of Cormantee (as I understood afterwards), were so weak as to believe any such thing, tho' many I had on board from other countries had that opinion.

"When the execution was over, I ordered the linguist to acquaint the men Negroes 'That now they might judge, no one that killed a white man should be spared.' And I thought proper now to acquaint them once for all, 'That if they attempted to mutiny again, I should be obliged to punish the ringleaders with death in order to prevent further mischief.' Upon this they all promised to be obedient, and I assured them they should be kindly used, if they kept their promise, which they faithfully did. For we sailed two days later from Anamaboe to Jamaica, and tho' they were on board nearly four months, from our going off the coast till they were sold at that island, they never gave us the least reason to be jealous of them, which doubtless was owing to the execution of the white man's murderer.

"These three mutinies I have here related are all that ever happened where I was present, tho' I have gone on many voyages to the Coast of Guinea. But I have heard of several that have ended in a very tragical manner. However, to avoid being tedious, I shall relate only one, which is very remarkable and happened on board the *Ferrers Galley* of London. Capt. Messervy, who, by his overcare and too great kindness to the Negroes on board his ship, was destroyed by them and the voyage at last came to nothing. I met this gentleman at Anamaboe on the Coast of Guinea in January, 1722. At his coming on board my ship, he informed me of his good fortune, in that he had purchased near 300 Negroes in a few days at a place called Cetre-Crue, on the windward part of the Coast of Guinea, which happened in this manner.

"It seems the inhabitants of this place, which lies near the seaside, had been often misused by some inland people, who for a long time had treated them in a villainous manner whenever they went to their towns with salt, or any other commodities to sell. For knowing the people of Cetre-Crue did in a great measure depend on them for their food, which is rice, they took their commodities and gave them just what quantity of rice they pleased in exchange. The Cetre-Crues having long complained of this injury, without redress, resolved to bear it no longer, but to revenge themselves by arms. And they were crowned with success, destroying and taking all the inhabitants of the principal town where they used to go and buy rice.

"Captain Messervy happened to anchor near Cetre-Crue just at that time, and had the opportunity of purchasing a great many of the captives at an easy rate. For the conquerors were glad to get something for them at that instant, since, if the ship had not been in the road, they would have been obliged to kill most of the man captives for their own security.

"After the captain had told me this story, he desired me to spare him some rice, having heard I had purchased a great many tuns to the windward, where he had bought little, not expecting to meet with so many slaves. This request I could not comply with, having provided no more than was necessary for my self, and for another of my owner's ships, which I quickly expected. And understanding from him that he had never been on the Coast of

Guinea before, I took the liberty to observe to him 'That as he had on board so many Negroes of one town and language, it required the utmost care and management to keep them from mutinying, and that I was sorry he had so little rice for them for I had experienced that the windward slaves are always very fond of it, it being their usual food in their own country, and he might certainly expect disatisfactions and uneasiness amongst them for want of a sufficient quantity.'

"This he took kindly, and having asked my advice about other matters, took his leave, inviting me to come next day to see him. I went accordingly on board his ship about three a clock in the afternoon. At four a clock the Negroes went to supper and Captain Messervy desired me to excuse him for a quarter of an hour, whilst he went forward to see the men Negroes served with victuals. I observed from the quarter deck that he himself put pepper and palm oyl amongst the rice that they were going to eat. When he came back to me, I could not forebear observing to him how imprudent it was in him to do so. For tho' it was proper for a commander sometimes to go forward and observe how things were managed, yet he ought to take a proper time and have a good many of his people in arms when he went, or else they having him so much in their power, might encourage the slaves to mutiny. For he might depend on it, they always aim at the chief person in the ship, whom they soon distinguish by the respect shown him by the rest of the people.

"He thanked me for this advice, but did not seem to relish it; saying he thought the old Proverb good 'That the master's eye makes the horse fat.' We then fell into other discourse and among the other things he told me he designed to go away in a few days. Accordingly he sailed three days after for Jamaica. Some months after I went for that place, where at my arrival, I found his ship and had the following melancholy account of his death, which happened about ten days after he left the Coast of Guinea . . .

"Being in the forecastle of the ship amongst the men Negroes when they were eating their victuals, they laid hold of him and beat out his brains with the little tubs out of which they eat their boiled rice. This mutiny having been plotted amongst all the grown Negroes on board, they run from the forepart of the ship in a body and endeavoured to force the barricado on the quarter deck, not regarding the musquets and halfpikes that were presented to their breasts by the white men through the loop-holes. So that at last the chief mate was obliged to order one of the quarter-deck guns laden with partridge shot, to be fired amongst them, which occasioned a terrible destruction. For there were near eighty Negroes kill'd and drowned, many jumping overboard when the gun was fired. This indeed put an end to the mutiny, but most of the slaves that remained alive grew so sullen that several of them were starved to death, obstinately refusing to take any sustenance. And after the ship was arrived at Jamaica, they attempted twice to mutiny before the sale of them began. This, with their former misbehaviour coming to be publickly known, none of the planters cared to buy them, tho' offered at a low price. So that this proved a very unsuccessful voyage, for the ship was detained many months at Jamaica on that account and last was lost there in a hurricane."

11

A CHANGE OF HEART
An Abolitionist Ship Captain

ALMOST FROM THE TIME men started taking slaves from the African coast facing the Atlantic, efforts were made to stop them. The first grumblings of a disturbed public conscience came in North America more than two centuries after the trade began. The English colonies had been populated by persons fleeing the oppressions of Europe, and they were the first to undertake an effective resistance to the spread of the inhumanities associated with slavery. Massachusetts and Rhode Island passed forms of antislavery laws in the mid-Seventeenth century. Some decades later, the Quakers of Germantown, Pennsylvania issued a strong resolution against slavery and the slave trade and it eventually was adopted by a number of other Quaker meetings in the Pennsylvania colony. The antislavery writings of the Pennsylvania Quakers were in a great measure responsible for swinging public opinion in America and Europe against the trade.

Virginia's House of Burgesses adopted a colonial law against the trade in the 1740's and a number of North American colonies repeatedly sent the English crown similar resolutions of opposition to the slave trade. They sent so many, in fact, that in 1770 King George III ordered them to desist from any move that would hurt the valued commerce.

Many colonists were personally unhappy with the trade and with slavery and freed their own slaves. But the slave trading interests in North America, which included the powerful New England shipping concerns and the Southern slave buyers and owners, effectively blocked any general ban on the trade for three decades after the Declaration of Independence. To preserve the union of new states, the antislavery leaders were reluctantly compelled to wait. Sentiment finally grew strong enough behind them to enable them to garner sufficient support in Congress to enact a law in 1807 prohibiting the import of slaves into the United States beginning January 1, 1808.

England was the real power in the trade, however, and it is to that nation's credit that she also became the leader in stopping it. Englishmen were not unanimous in support of repeal, by any means, and it took decades of fierce infighting to turn public opinion against the entrenched and vicious slave trading forces.

One of the most important victories in the humanitarian movement was the ruling by Lord Justice Mansfield in 1772 in a case brought by Granville Sharp of London. Sharp had nursed an abandoned, sick slave back to health, only to have the original owner reclaim him. Sharp then became infuriated when he was unable to rescue the slave, and brought a test case with another fugitive slave in a deliberate attack on England's slave-owning laws. Mansfield ruled that once a slave set foot on English soil he immediately became free. Though the ruling meant the abolition of slavery in England, it did not affect the slave trade or slave ownership in British colonial possessions.

To attack the trade itself a small corps of reformers had several years earlier set out to turn public opinion against it. Their efforts were ineffective, however, because they lacked facts, figures and virtually any basic knowledge about the trade, except that they personally felt it to be evil. They were unable to convince many others without more proof. Here was a desperate need for action and as history has proven time and again, when man reaches a point of such despair, active men of courage will somehow be found. Such men were Thomas Clarkson and William Wilberforce and their companions in the Abolition Society.

In 1785, Thomas Clarkson, a young student at Cambridge University, decided to enter a Latin essay contest. The theme of his essay was to be slavery. He knew nothing of the subject but in his studies he ran across the writings of Anthony Benezet, a French-born Pennsylvania Quaker who had written books and pamphlets on the evils of slavery.

Clarkson became incensed by what he read, wrote a soul-stirring essay which won the contest, and then set out on a life-long career to kill the trade. At first he believed it was to be a one-man David-and-Goliath battle, but then he learned of a small group of reformers with the same goal. He activated a dormant Quaker committee formed earlier to combat slavery and in 1787, Clarkson, Sharp and others organized the Society for the Abolition of the Slave Trade.

A poor public speaker, Clarkson nevertheless had boundless drive. Seeing the need for evidence of the trade's rottenness, he set out to get it. He went to Liverpool, England's chief slaving port, Bristol and anywhere he could corner a person who could provide the first-hand information he wanted. He was attacked and beaten by thugs hired by slave ship owners and traders whose livelihoods depended on the slave commerce. The harassed zealot continued with his self-appointed mission and eventually persuaded ship captains and sailors, surgeons and pursers to tell of the horrors they had witnessed. Many of these were later to refute their testimony, and a number vanished as the strength of the slave trade interests was brought to bear in a vain effort to muzzle the abolitionists. But Clarkson already had enough information to provide the foundation for others to launch their attack in Parliament.

William Wilberforce, the frail son of a Yorkshire merchant, and the Member of Parliament for Hull, was enlisted by the Abolition Society to present its case in the House of Commons. A militant Christian, Wilberforce immediately accepted the offer to champion the cause and became a foe of the slave trade for the rest of his days.

The society launched a campaign to arouse the public and by 1789 had published thousands of books and pamphlets and sold Wedgwood's pottery bearing the society's seal, a Negro in chains. Liverpool and slavery interests countered viciously. The abolitionists were slandered openly and malicious rumors circulated to smear their reputations. The ports and slave merchants cried loudly that the trade was the base of English commerce and stopping it would throw thousands out of work. They circulated the writings of a Church of England priest, a former Jesuit, who argued that the trade and slavery were sanctioned by God, according to his Biblical research.

In 1788, the crown appointed a committee of the Privy Council to hold hearings on the slave trade. The result was a law that year limiting the number of slaves which could be taken by a vessel on a rate based on its tonnage. The law also regulated conditions aboard to insure better health for the slaves.

In 1789, Parliament began a three-year investigation of the trade and a Parliamentary committee interviewed dozens of eyewitnesses, most of them lined up by the abolitionists. In 1791, Wilberforce proposed a bill to abolish the trade. It was defeated 163 to 88. He tried again and again in succeeding years, during which time slavery was a constant subject of debate in Parliament, but each time he was defeated. His failure was largely the result of a sharp turn to conservatism in 1792, brought on by the violence of the revolution in France. In 1806, however, the conservative government was replaced and in the spring of 1807

Prime Minister William Grenville presented a bill effecting the trade's end. This time it passed.

As the last vote was cast in the House of Commons on the historic bill marking the death of the legal trade, Wilberforce collapsed in weeping exhaustion. His fellow MP's gave him, as he was carried from the floor, one of the most tumultuous ovations ever heard in the House.

Wilberforce, Clarkson, Sharp and the other leaders in the abolitionist movement deserve the greatest tributes for their devotion to the cause of elimination of slavery. But there were many of lesser renown in the movement and who, in their own ways, were as important and courageous in the long fight. One of these, oddly enough, was a former slave ship captain and thus one of the few actively in the movement who had seen the evils of the trade firsthand.

John Newton, author and composer of the famed Olney Hymns, was a sailor and commander of slave ships for many years before turning to the ministry and joining forces with those out to quell his former livelihood. His observations were considered of high value by the reformers.

Newton was born in London in 1725, the son of a sea captain engaged in the Mediterranean mercantile trade. His mother died when he was seven and Newton spent his childhood in schools designed to prepare him for the ministry, or at least imbue him with a stern, pious outlook. He made several voyages with his father, then was sent to a pre-ministry school, from which his unruly temperament forced his removal within a few months. When Newton was sixteen, a friend of his father arranged a voyage to the West Indies for the youth. Newton rapidly turned to the dissolute life of a sailor and caroused his way from port to port.

His father disapproved, but Newton continued in his wanton, rebellious voyaging. Finally, on one trip his ship was wrecked on the African coast and he fell into the hands of a white trader who treated him as a slave. The trader's Negro mistress delighted in tormenting the young Englishman. Newton said that when he was bedridden in illness, he was kept alive only by the trader's slaves who smuggled him food.

In February 1747, a ship sent out by his father rescued him. In the homeward voyage, the vessel almost foundered off Newfoundland. Newton said that except for the superhuman exertions of the crew to keep the ship afloat, they would have perished. While the outcome was still in doubt, Newton prayed to God, whom he had almost forsaken. The ship stayed afloat and finally came to anchor in a safe harbor.

Newton attributed his salvation to the Divine Will and while the ship was being refitted, he went to church and received the Sacrament, for the first time in years. How deep was his religious reconversion is undetermined. Two years later he sailed for Sierra Leone as mate on a slaver.

He wrote a friend from the African coast: "Though we have been here for six months I have not been ten days in the ship, being continually cruising about in the boats to purchase souls, for which we are obliged to take as much pains as the Jesuits are said to do in making proselytes, sometimes venturing in a little canoe through seas like mountains, sometimes traveling through the woods, often in danger from the wild beasts, and much oftener from the more wild inhabitants, scorched by the sun in the day and chilled by the dews in the night."*

That Newton may have regarded himself as a missionary of sorts is also undetermined, but there was little doubt he faced the perils of his trade.

"Several boats in the same time were cut off [by natives]; several white men poisoned, and in my own boat I buried six or seven people with fevers. When going on shore, or returning from

* Williams, *Liverpool Privateers*. London, 1897.

it, in their little canoes, I have been more than once or twice over-set by the violence of the surf, or break of the sea, and brought to land half dead, for I could not swim."

He sailed to Antigua, from there to Charleston, South Carolina and returned to Liverpool in December 1749. In February 1750, he married Mary Catlett, a childhood sweetheart. The following August, Newton sailed from Liverpool as commander of the slave ship *Duke of Argyle.* In his letters to his wife, he tried to describe his position as slave ship captain.

"I am as absolute in my small dominions as any potentate in Europe. If I say to one, come, he comes; if to another, go, he flies. If I order one person to do something, perhaps three or four will be ambitious of a share in the service. Not a man in the ship will eat his dinner till I please to give him leave. Nay, nobody dares to say it is twelve or eight o'clock, in my hearing, till I think proper to say so first.

"There is a mighty bustle of attendance when I leave the ship, and a strict watch kept while I am absent, lest I should return unawares, and not be received in due form. And should I stay till midnight (which for that reason I never do without necessity) nobody must presume to shut their eyes until they have had the honour of seeing me again. I would have you judge from my manner of relating these ceremonies, that I do not value them highly for their own sake; but they are old-fashioned customs and necessary to be kept up, for without a strict discipline the common sailors would be unmanageable."

At one time in his first voyage as captain, Newton met the Negress who had tormented him nearly to his grave. His revenge was sweet, but charitable. He invited her aboard his ship, and when she recognized him, she was terrified. Newton, however, gave her presents and sent her ashore unharmed.

Newton told a friend that as commander of a slave ship, with a number of women under his absolute command, he was well aware of the danger of the situation and resolved to abstain from meat and drink nothing stronger than water during the voyage across the Atlantic.

He reached home in November 1751, and sailed again in July 1752, as commander of the new slave ship, the *African.* Again at sea, he established religious services aboard his ship, setting aside daily periods for prayer. His crew may have regarded the new regimen as an imposition or an indication of their skipper's weakness. Newton relates of his adventures:

"In the course of this voyage I was wonderfully preserved in the midst of many obvious and unforeseen dangers. At one time there was a conspiracy amongst my own people to turn pirates and take the ship from me. When the plot was nearly ripe, and they only waited a convenient opportunity, two of those concerned in it were taken ill in one day. One of them died, and he was the only person I buried while on board. This suspended the affair, and opened a way to its discovery, or the consequences might have been fatal. The slaves on board were likewise frequently plotting insurrections and were sometimes upon the very brink of mischief, but it was always disclosed in due time. When I have thought myself most secure, I have been suddenly alarmed with danger; when I have almost despaired of life, as sudden a deliverance has been vouchsafed to me. My stay upon the coast was long, the trade very precarious, and in the pursuit of my business, on board and on shore, I was near death often."

On one occasion he had a dream and a premonition of danger if he went ashore. The next day he was supposed to go but didn't, and shortly learned that a trader had plotted to attack him for a suspected intrigue of which Newton maintained he was innocent.

Newton's religious bent strongly patterned his life aboard ship and in a letter to his wife he wrote of his "Sea Sunday."

"The Saturday evening is a time of devotion when I especially beg a blessing on your Sunday, as I know, where you are, you are unavoidably exposed to trifling company. I usually rise at four o'clock in the morning, and after seeking a blessing on the day, take a serious walk on the deck. Then I read two or three select chapters. At breakfast, I eat and drink more than I talk, for I have no one here to join in such conversation as I then choose. At the hour of your going to Church I attend you in my mind with another prayer; and at eleven o'clock the ship's bell rings my own little congregation about me. To them I read the morning service according to the Liturgy. Then I walk the deck and attend my observation (take the latitude of the ship). After dinner a brief rest, or I write in my diary, I think again upon you at the time of afternoon service, and once more assemble the crew for worship. I take tea at four, then follows a Scripture lesson, and a walk and a private devotion at six."

In August 1754, Newton completed another long voyage as a captain and in summary he wrote:

"I had the pleasure to return thanks in the churches (at Liverpool) for an African voyage performed without any accident or the loss of a single man; and it was much noticed and acknowledged in the town. I question if it is not the only instance of the kind. When I made my first appearance upon the Exchange, a stranger would have thought me a person of great importance, by the various congratulations I received from almost every gentleman present."

"My stay at home was intended to be but short, and by the beginning of November I was ready again for the sea, but the Lord saw fit to overrule my design." Two days before he was to leave, he was taken ill and on the advice of his physicians he resigned his command.

Newton saw the illness and his forced resignation as the answer to a prayer. "During the time I was engaged in the slave trade, I never had the least scruple as to its lawfulness. I was, upon the whole, satisfied with it, as the appointment Providence had marked out for me; yet it was in many respects far from eligible. It is, indeed, accounted a genteel employment, and is usually very profitable, though to me it did not prove so, the Lord seeing that a large increase of wealth could not be good for me. However, I considered myself as a sort of gaoler or turnkey; and I was sometimes shocked with an employment that was perpetually conversant with chains, bolts and shackles. In this view, I had often petitioned in my prayers that the Lord (in His own time) would be pleased to fix me in a more humane calling, and (if it might be) place me where I might have more frequent converse with His people and ordinances, and be freed from those long separations from home, which very often were hard to bear."

Newton subsequently was given a sinecure as tide surveyor at Liverpool. His thoughts turned to entering the ministry and nearly ten years later he accepted the curacy of Olney. He was thirty-nine at the time. One of his closest friends there was the poet William Cowper, whose appeals against slavery won him fame.

From Olney, Newton went to two London parishes and there repeatedly spoke out against the slave trade. In 1763, he wrote a statement which indicated his compulsion to indict the trade and assuage his own involvement.

"I felt greatly the disagreeableness of the business. The office of a gaoler, and the restraints under which I was obliged to keep my prisoners, were not suitable to my feelings. But I considered the line of life which God in His providence had allotted me, as a cross which I ought to bear with patience and thankfulness till he should be pleased to deliver me from it. Till then I only thought myself bound to treat the slaves under my care with gentleness, and to consult their ease and convenience so far as was consistent with the safety of the whole family of whites and blacks on board my ship."

He wrote in 1791: "I consider myself bound in conscience to

bear my testimony at least, and to wash my hands from the guilt, which, if persisted in now that things have been so thoroughly investigated and brought to light, will, I think constitute a national sin of a scarlet and crimson dye."

The remarks of the former slave ship captain were published in pamphlets and circulated widely. From all parts of the world, Newton received letters commending him for his stand. But Newton disclaimed any credit. On one occasion, he refused a doctorate degree from the University of New Jersey and adamantly returned unopened letters addressed to him as "Dr. Newton."

Newton was an important witness before the Parliamentary committees investigating the slave trade, openly supplying them firsthand information from his years in the business.

"If my testimony should not be necessary or serviceable, I am bound in conscience to take shame to myself by a public confession, which, however sincere, comes too late to prevent or repair the misery and mischief to which I have formerly been accessory. I hope it always will be a subject of humiliating reflection to me that I was once an active instrument in a business at which my heart now shudders.

"Perhaps what I have said of myself may be applicable to the nation at large. The slave trade was always unjustifiable. But inattention and interest prevented for a time the evil from being perceived. It is otherwise at present. The mischiefs and evils connected with it have been of late years represented with such undeniable evidence, and are now so generally known, that hardly an objection can be made to the almost universal wish for the suppression of this trade, save on the ground of political expedience."

After the initial defeats in Parliament to rid the nation of the slave ships, Newton heatedly appealed to Englishmen's consciences. In a sermon in 1794, he said: "There is a cry of blood against us — a cry accumulated by the accession of fresh victims, of thousands, of scores of thousands . . . of hundreds of thousands from year to year."

In 1797, he preached: "If the trade is at present carried on to the same extent and nearly in the same manner, while we are delaying from year to year to put a stop to our part in it, the blood of many thousands of our helpless, much injured fellow creatures is crying against us. The pitiable state of the survivors who are torn from their relatives, connections, and their native land must be taken into account. Enough of this horrid scene. I fear the African trade is a national sin, for the enormities which accompany it are now generally known."

In 1804, when he was seventy-nine, Newton confided to a friend that "for 40 years past I have thought every waking hour of my former misery."

Newton died on December 19, 1807, the year that brought the end to the English slave trade. He lived to see the commerce as a legitimate business halted. For an epitaph on his tombstone, he chose only: "John Newton, Clerk, Once an Infidel and Libertine, A Servant of Slaves . . ."

12

YEARS OF THE SLAVE SMUGGLERS

ABOLITIONISTS on both sides of the Atlantic naively assumed that laws against the slave trade would stop it. Entirely the opposite occurred, however. Slave shipping turned into a thriving sub rosa commerce of piracy and smuggling. Every kind of ruffian and scoundrel of the seven seas joined in it. To the plantation owners of the West Indies, these rogue mariners became soldiers of fortune, helping them to combat what they considered a madness inflicted on them by the governments of Europe and North America.

The demand for slaves increased in the Western Hemisphere as the industrial revolution grew apace. The manufacturing centers of North America and Europe developed a ravenous appetite for raw materials, and especially for the cheap sugar and cotton produced on the slave plantations. Africa still had a huge surplus of people and despite the laws aimed at cutting off the trade, the white man's man-buying businesses on the African coast were still open. A quick profit was ready and waiting for the men willing to take the risks. The value of a prime field hand, for example, tripled in the Caribbean slave marts in the first two decades after abolition. He could be bought in Africa for as low as $20 and sold in New Orleans for up to $2,500. A quick successful trip past the naval patrols could net a smuggler several hundred thousand dollars.

Britain led the van of nations in policing the Atlantic but her success in halting the contraband trade was limited. It was no easy matter to bottle up three thousand miles of coast to slave ships. The African patrol squadrons were small cruisers, few in number and were no match for the fast, sleek ships the slavers began using. Later, steam cruisers were added to the African patrols but for most of the decades of their battle to suppress the trade, the naval commanders had to use ships and equipment which were years behind in design and development to those used by the slavers.

The wily slaver soon learned too to keep one jump ahead of the law, which in itself was often vague and laden with complex treaty agreements which changed constantly with political conditions in Europe. It was a game of hide-and-seek, and when pursued, a slaver could note the nationality of the pursuing cruiser, hoist the flag of a nation the cruiser was not empowered to search and sail away safely. Many ships maintained two or more sets of registries, often two captains, one for each flag.

As the naval patrols increased their vigilance, the small operators were shut down. Slave shipping, clandestine as it had to be, required heavy investments to outfit a ship in secret, bribe port officials at all points along the voyage, hire expensive rogues to sail it, and then pay for the costly arrangements to sneak the slaves on and off the ship on each coast. A small-timer could ill afford the loss of a ship and cargo to the navy.

Until the equipment clauses were included in treaties in the 1840's, the patrolling navies could seize ships only when they had slaves on board. This left an obvious way out for the desperate slaver when cornered. The *Brillante* incident during this period illustrates this "last resort" used by one ship captain. The story about the *Brillante* has never been substantiated but because of its wide acceptance at the time, it presumably had a thread of truth.*

The *Brillante*, a loaded slave brig captained by a man named Homans, reportedly was pursued and ultimately trapped by four British cruisers late one afternoon. The sea was still, the wind died away and there was no apparent avenue of escape for Homans and his ship.

Night came as the Britishers began to close in. Under cover of darkness, Homans had his crew quickly haul out the ship's largest anchor and long lenghts of cable chain which he had stretched around the ship at the rail. Then he had the six hundred slaves on board brought on deck and bound to the anchor cable by strong cords to their manacles. Soon the grind of oar locks and faint splash of oar blades warned Homans of the approaching boats of the British cruisers. At a signal from Homans, the rope binding the anchor was cut. Suddenly the air was filled with shrieks and screams. There was a low rumble, a long, drawn-out splash, and then the sea and the ship were quiet again. When the boarders reached the *Brillante*, the smell of slaves hung heavily on the ship. Huge kettles cooking food for the slaves were still cooling. Manacles and other slave equipment were on deck, but there was not a single slave left on board as evidence. Homans and his crew, jeering smiles on their faces, went free.

Equipment clauses of the various treaties empowered the navies to seize slavers if slave shipping equipment was on board, though slaves were not . . . This included hatches with open grating instead of closed hatches normally found on merchant vessels, spare planking for slave decks, shackles or handcuffs, unusually large cooking boilers and food supplies, matting, water casks or tubs.

Life in the African naval squadrons was one of monotony, frustration, disease and the occasional excitement of a chase. The

* Spears, *American Slave Trade*. London, 1900.

laws governing seizure of a ship were so involved that naval commanders had to proceed with special care to avoid legal entanglement with one of the Mixed Commissions to which he had to take his prizes. A false seizure, or one so judged by the commission, could end up with a commander being assessed heavy damages and the slaver going free. Captured slaves were taken to one of the free colonies established on the African coast and there liberated. Sierra Leone, established first by the abolitionists in 1787 as a refuge for freed slaves, was taken over as a Crown Colony in 1808 and a prize court located there. The colony inspired the American free settlement of Liberia immediately to the south and the French colony at Libreville to the northeast.

Getting a seized slaver back to port was no easy job. It meant manning it with a prize crew of a handful of sailors under the command of a junior officer, sometimes only a midshipman. They had to sail the ship and cope with the captured as well. The *Felicidade* incident illustrated to the world the danger inherent in this job.

The *Felicidade*, a Brazilian slaver, was captured equipped but empty by the British cruiser *Wasp* in 1845. A midshipman and nine crewmen were put aboard to take the slaver to port. But once the *Wasp* was out of sight, the slaver's crew mutinied, killed the Englishmen and threw their bodies overboard. Some days later the *Felicidade* was boarded again, this time by the British cruiser *Star*, which naturally knew nothing of the earlier episode.

On a search of the *Felicidade*, a book belonging to the midshipman was found. At this, a Brazilian crewman confessed that his shipmates had slain the *Wasp*'s prize crew. Ten of the Brazilians were taken to England, tried for murder, and convicted. But on an appeal to a higher court, their attorneys argued that the *Felicidade* had been seized illegally, in view that there were no slaves aboard at the time, and they won a reversal. The court also ruled that the freed Brazilians should be taken back to their country at British expense.

The effect of this ruling on British public opinion was explosive. It created such a furor against the slave trade that the cry "Remember the *Felicidade*" became a rallying cry for boarding parties attacking slave ships.

Diseases riddled the crews of the African cruisers during the long, hot patrols. An epidemic of what was believed to be yellow fever reduced the crew of the H.M.S. *Eden* from one hundred thirty-five to twelve in a four-month period. One of the most foolhardy steps to prove this disease was not contagious was taken by the surgeon of the H.M.S. *Sybille* in 1830. He collected a glass of black vomit from seamen sick with the fever, flamboyantly toasted a fellow officer and drank it down. As the crew gathered around to watch him die, he strolled the quarterdeck until dinner time, then went to his meal as fit as ever, or so the story goes. Whether he survived the journey has never been recorded. In 1854, quinine was introduced and health conditions began to improve in the squadrons assigned to the tropics.

Naval strategies changed through the years as more funds for squadrons were allocated, antitrade laws strengthened and sympathy swung behind suppression. From offshore patrolling aimed at snaring loaded slavers, naval cruisers in the 1840's began close inshore blockades of slave ports. They finally resorted to raids to destroy slave stations.

The Brazilian trade flourished during this period. Under an agreement reached in 1826, Britain seized only Brazilian ships carrying slaves north of the equator, and not until 1845 did the traffic "south of the line" come under attack. Later in that decade British cruisers cracked down hard on Brazilian slavers and brought the trade nearly to a standstill for a while — although slave ships continued to ply the Atlantic to Brazil until the 1880's. As everywhere else, slave shipping into a nation continued until slavery itself was abolished within the nation or colony — in British colonies in 1833, French in 1848, the American states in the 1860's and Brazil in 1888. There is no date marking the end of slave shipping, though the last decade of significant activity was the 1850's. British warships were withdrawn from the patrol during the Crimean War and the slave traffic across the ocean took an upswing until they returned. The American squadron and American slave shipping as well were withdrawn during the Civil War and British squadrons squelched most of the shipping that was left.

The years following the official abolition in 1808 of the slave trade by the United States was a shameful period for the new nation. Its pride was threatened and so it had to fight another expensive war in 1812 with England. With little trust in its former ruler, the United States had steadfastly refused the British any "right to search" American vessels on the high seas, whether slavers or not. Americans loftily regarded the British zeal as a cover hiding a real intent to keep legitimate merchants of other nations, particularly American, from trading on foreign coasts. Secretary of State John Quincy Adams, though a dedicated opponent of the slave trade, said that to permit foreign officers the right to search American vessels "would be making slaves of ourselves." But later, as President, Adams agreed to support the African patrol and sent four small warships to help the British on the Guinea Coast. Until this time, many Americans had denied that their flag was being used as a cover by slavers, but the tiny American squadron soon proved them wrong. The British maintained that much of the slave traffic was being carried by ships flying American flags, and there was no denying the truth in their charge once official American observers arrived on the scene.*

But with half of the new nation composing an important slave buying market, and part of the other half, the New England states,

---

* Andrew Hull Foote, *Africa and the American Flag*. New York, 1862.

having a vested interest in such profitable maritime affairs, American participation in stopping the trade was half-hearted at best. It was not until the Webster–Ashburton Treaty of 1842 that the United States, goaded by the British, agreed to beef up its African squadron and step up its suppressive efforts along its own shores. A Southern Congressman about this time charged heatedly that apathy toward the trade was not wholly below the Mason–Dixon line, as many Northerners maintained. Southerners, he said, were only receivers of goods stolen by Northerners. To appease the nonmaritime Northerners earnestly trying to halt the traffic, Congress during this period passed anti–slave trading laws, then declined to appropriate funds to carry them out, thus soothing Northern shipping interests and Southern slave holders.

Thomas Buchanan, governor of Liberia in 1840, provides a window on American shipping in the African slave trade during the summer of 1839. In a report to the U.S. Secretary of Navy, subsequently published in the *Army and Navy Chronicle*, he listed the following ships, and shows positively that the evil of slave shipping was far from over.*

"The *Venus*, of Baltimore, a ship of 460 tons, sailed in April (1839) with 860 slaves on board, for Havana, Wm. Phillips, master. She is now (in November) reported to be back on the coast, fully armed, and prepared for resistance. On her last voyage she cleared, after paying all expenses, $200,000.

"The *Traveller*, a Baltimore schooner, after coasting here for some weeks, collecting rice, etc., for the factories, sailed in May, with a full cargo of slaves for Havana. She is reported to be again on the coast.

"The *Wyoming*, captured by H.B.M. Brig *Buzzard*, and sent to the U.S.

"The *Eagle*, of Baltimore, sent home by a British cruiser.

"In April, two American schooners were sent into Sierra Leone

* *Army and Navy Chronicle*, February 13, 1840.

by H.B.M. brigs *Lyle* and *Saracen*, completely refitted for the slave trade; the court would not receive them on account of their being Americans.

"The *Hugh Boyle*, of Baltimore, a schooner of 120 tons, sailed in the spring with 120 slaves on board. She returned a short time since from Havana, and about the middle of October sailed again for the Gallinas with a full cargo of slaves on board.

"The *Mary Ann Cassard* was taken, fitted for the slave trade, and sent into Sierra Leone by Lieutenant Kellar of H.B.M. brig *Brisk*. The court would not receive her, and Lieut. Kellar was merged with damages for violating the American flag. Two weeks after, she was taken with more than 200 slaves.

"The *Iago* was taken up by the *Termagant*, and carried into Sierra Leone, completely fitted for slaves. The court refused to receive her. Not long afterwards she was taken by the *Saracen*, just as she was about to receive her slaves on board; she had made way with the American flag and papers, and had the Spanish up at the time, consequently she was condemned and cut up.

"The *Euphrates*, of Baltimore, was taken by Lord F. Russell, delivered to me in July, and sent to Philadelphia in August.

"The *Jack Wilding*, of Baltimore, schooner, Wm. Young, commander, taken in British Acra, full cargo and 1100 doubloons, by H.B.M. brig *Dolphin*.

"The *Waukeen*, captured in New Cesters, in July. Then under Spanish, but a short time under American colors (of New Orleans).

"The *Victoria*, of New Orleans, on this coast during most of the summer, under American colors, doing business for the slavers. She sailed here with about 400 slaves, and was captured under Spanish colors at St. Jago de Cuba, with 270 on board, the rest having perished.

"The *Rebecca*, of Baltimore, taken under Spanish colors and sent into Sierra Leone, and condemned. Her American papers and flag were found on board her, with a letter from her owner, J. Murphy, of Baltimore, directing the captain how to proceed, to destroy the American colors and papers when the slaves should be received . . .

"The *George Cook*, of Baltimore, Wm. Weems, master, sailed in September from Kabendo, with 320 slaves on board.

"The *Butterfly*, American brigantine, captured in British waters and carried into Sierra Leone.

"*My Boy*, a schooner of New Orleans. Last year she sailed from the coast with a full cargo of slaves. In October last year she was captured at British Acra, fitted for the slave trade, J. Harvey, master.

"*Charleston*, of Charleston, sailed from the Gallinas in January last with 308 slaves.

"*Hyperion*, of Baltimore, Wm. Hackland, master, some time on the coast under American colors, in November 1838, she was taken under Spanish colors and condemned.

"*Mary Cushing*, of Baltimore, once taken, was brought into Sierra Leone, and cleared on account of her American character; in October 1839, she was captured with 427 slaves on board — captain, American.

"*Sarah and Priscilla*, schooner, of Baltimore, taken at Gallinas, completed fitted for the slave trade, carried into Sierra Leone — cleared on account of her American character."

13

MUTINY TO FREEDOM

NOT ALL SLAVE MUTINIES on shipboard were unsuccessful. There are at least two successful slave mutinies which became etched on American history as benchmarks on the tormented road toward Negro freedom. One, the *Creole* uprising, provoked such a confrontation between the United States and Great Britain that some American Congressmen gloomily predicted it would lead to a total war in the civilized world.

The second, the mutiny aboard the schooner *Amistad*, became a cause célèbre for abolitionists and led to what has been referred as the "trial of one president by another."

The brig *Creole* of Richmond, Virginia, set sail from its wharf on the James River port in mid-October 1841, bound for New Orleans. Downriver at Norfolk, one hundred thirty-five slaves, destined for the slave block in the Crescent City, were added to the *Creole*'s cargo of tobacco.* William Merritt, the white superintendent who would accompany the blacks to their destination, herded them aboard in single file. Some of the Negroes were crying at leaving their old plantation homes, where they had enjoyed the only happiness they knew, such as it was. Others wept because they were being separated from husband, children, parents and

* William Jay, *The* Creole *Case*. New York, 1842.

[222]

their other kin. Except for those lucky enough to be purchased for house help, the slaves were bound for the grueling labor of the Louisiana and Mississippi cane fields.

One among them was different. A large man, Madison Washington did not wear his bondage with silent indifference or submissiveness. Washington had escaped from his Virginia master once, gone north, but had returned to help his wife escape also. He was recaptured in the attempt and, because of his recalcitrance, consigned to Merritt for the penultimate punishment — sale as a cane hand.

The *Creole* sailed from Hampton Roads on the tide of October 27. The men were loaded in the forward hold, the women and children aft. The hogsheads of tobacco were between them. On the evening of November 7, when the ship was off the coast of Florida, Washington crept out of the men's compartment and made his way unseen to the women's. Another slave sought to do the same, but the deck watch caught him. Perhaps to prevent harsher punishment, he told the guard Washington had gone ahead. Merritt was summoned and he went immediately to the women's compartment. When he entered, Washington bolted through the door. In the confusion on deck, the other slave seized a pistol and fired, wounding the ship's mate slightly. The two slaves on deck realized the ultimate crisis had come. Wounding a white man meant their death, unless they acted quickly. Washington shouted for the slaves below to help seize the ship.

The struggle was joined instantly by seventeen other blacks who poured out of the hold. The alarm was sounded by the guard and the mate, but one by one, the crew was subdued. Despite the ferocity of the fight, however, only one man was killed — a seaman named Hewell who rushed at a group of slaves with a musket. In the scuffle, he was stabbed.

Seeing their success, Washington instantly took command, and demanded that the violence stop. According to one account,

"Two of the sailors were wounded and their wounds were dressed by the Negroes. The captain also was injured, and he was put into the forehold and his wounds dressed, and his wife, child and niece were unmolested. It does not appear that the blacks committed a single act of robbery, or treated their captives with the slightest unnecessary harshness; and they declared at the time, that 'All they had done was for their freedom'."*

The slave dealer Merritt had hidden in his cabin under a pile of blankets, using as his sentinel a woman slave named Mary. The mutineers found him and pulled him on deck, and would have slain him but for Mary's pleading that his life be spared. Washington ordered Merritt then to choose — his life and serve as their navigator, or be slain. Merritt wasted no time in choosing the former and at Washington's direction, headed the ship for Nassau, British territory and freedom, as every slave knew.

The *Creole* arrived at the port of Nassau on November 9. Washington was smart enough to know he had to deal with officialdom, so he asked British authorities to come aboard to help the Negroes. The captain and his family and the whites aboard were permitted to go ashore. With the British came the American Consul, who immediately demanded the mutineers be imprisoned for return to the United States and trial for mutiny and murder.

Herein began a paradox that provoked the international dispute. British law said anyone who set foot on British territory was automatically free. The British magistrates who went aboard the *Creole* had Washington and his eighteen compatriots imprisoned in connection with "mutiny and murder." But they had never had a case like the *Creole*'s and they weren't certain what to do about the other slaves still aboard.

Merritt demanded they be held and returned to the United States as his property. The British governor then sent a troop of

* Jay, *The* Creole *Case*.

soldiers on board the *Creole* to take the mutineers ashore and
see that the slaves didn't escape. But along with the magistrates
and the soldiers came a small fleet of boats manned by Nassau
residents who took a personal interest in the *Creole* slaves. As the
magistrates deliberated, tension in the boats mounted. Fearing
bloodshed, the magistrates ruled that mutineers would be held,
but the others were to be considered passengers and could go
ashore if they chose. With great excitement, the unconfined *Creole*
slaves went over the sides into welcoming arms of the Nassauans
in the boats below. They were taken ashore, but the Nassau pro-
tectors, still fearing a reversal, chartered a small ship and had
the freed Negroes spirited to Jamaica beyond reach.

Ironically, the nineteen mutineers, looking in scorn at those who
had done nothing to fight for their freedom, were rowed ashore
in irons and held there while the British sent for direction from
London. Daniel Webster, then U.S. Secretary of State, wrote
immediately from Washington to the American minister in London to present the case for return of the *Creole* slave cargo, "with
a distinct declaration, that, if the facts turned out as stated, the
government thinks it a clear case of indemnification." The American government's view was that the slaves had committed a crime
and deserved punishment.*

But England took a different view. With the support of Parliament, the British leaders stiffly responded that the *Creole* Negroes must "stand or fall by British laws only." They said there
was no authority to surrender the fugitives nor hold in custody the
mutineers. The Admiralty Court in Nassau then ruled that Madison Washington and his companions were free men and that they
were justified in the measures they took to gain their freedom.*

The reverberations of the case continued in the United States.

* W. O. Blake, *The History of Slavery and the Slave Trade.* Columbus, Ohio,
1858.

In Congress, Representative Joshua R. Giddings of Ohio took up the cause of the *Creole* slaves and presented resolutions saying that once the *Creole* had left Virginia, a slave state, the slaves were subject to United States law only and the slaves thus violated no United States law "in securing their natural rights to personal liberty." In addition, he said that all attempts to re-enslave them would be unauthorized by the Constitution.

Slavery interests, very powerful in the young nation, saw these words as threatening coastwise shipping of slaves and proslavery congressmen began a bitter and personal attack on Giddings. His opponents said Giddings's resolution touched "a subject of negotiation between the United States and Great Britain of a most delicate nature" and could possibly involve "those nations and the whole civilized world in war."

A resolution of condemnation of Giddings was introduced and so heated became feelings that fellow House members refused even to permit Giddings to defend himself. Giddings rose and presented an eloquent and bitter castigation of his enemies. "Mr. Speaker, I stand before the House in a peculiar situation. It is proposed to pass a vote of censure upon me, substantially for the reason that I differ in the opinion from the majority of the members.

"The vote is about to be taken without giving me time to be heard. It would be idle for me to say that I am ignorant of the disposition of the majority to pass the resolution [of censure]. I have been violently assailed in a personal manner, but have had no opportunity of being heard in reply. I do not now stand here to ask for any favor or to crave any mercy at the hands of the members. But in the name of an insulted constituency — in behalf of the people of these states and the federal constitution — I demand a hearing, agreeably to the rights guaranteed to me, and in the ordinary mode of proceeding. I accept of no other privilege; I will receive no other courtesy."

His challenge to reason and fairness went unheeded. The vote was 125 to 69 against him. Giddings promptly resigned and left immediately for Ohio. There the governor called an immediate special election and Giddings was re-elected by a large majority. On May 5, he reclaimed his seat in Congress, fully vindicated by the people he served.*

The *Amistad* mutiny served as a rallying issue for the abolitionists, and in the years before the Civil War the leader of the mutineers, Joseph Cinquez, was lionized by the antislavery advocates. The ordeal of the *Amistad* began with a group of slaves in Africa and ended in the Supreme Court of the United States with a former President pitted against the one in office.

On August 18, 1839, a long, low black schooner appeared off New York harbor.† It veered away, then two days later reappeared. Two pilot boats approached the ship. The first saw a bedraggled group of Negroes peering at them from the rails. The pilot boat crew gave the blacks some apples. When the second boat came closer, the Negroes became frightened and sailed away.

Six days later, the same long, low black schooner anchored near Montauk Point at the tip of Long Island, and a group of the Negroes aboard came ashore for supplies. As they sat in the sand talking with a party of whites, using hand signals and signs drawn in the sand, the U.S. Navy brig *Washington*, making routine soundings in the vicinity, came slowly around the point. Its captain, thinking the schooner a pirate, immediately sent a party of sailors aboard to seize it.

Thus the two-month-long sea voyage of the Spanish schooner *Amistad*, commanded by a desperate crew of mutinous slaves who thought they were going to Africa and ended up in New York, came to an end. The *Washington* took the *Amistad* and

* Blake, *Slavery and the Slave Trade.*
† John Warner Barber, *A History of the* Amistad *Captives.* New Haven, 1840.

its wretched-looking crew to New London, Connecticut, where the leader, Joseph Cinquez, and his thirty-eight fellow Africans were charged with mutiny and murder.*

Unable to speak a word of English or Spanish, the slaves could communicate with the Americans only through the *Amistad*'s cabin boy, Antonio, the Negro slave of the schooner's captain. Antonio and two Spaniards found on board the *Amistad* on its capture were all that was left of the *Amistad*'s passengers and crew. The Spaniards and Antonio told their own versions of what had happened. The Spaniards said they owned the *Amistad* Negroes and demanded the slaves be returned to Cuba in irons and be tried for mutiny and murder. To further the Africans' plight, the captain of the *Washington*, following the custom of naval vessels that seized pirates or slave ships, filed suit for a share of salvage damages against the *Amistad* and the slaves.

The blacks huddled in misery in the Connecticut jail while the law further entangled them. The blacks were jailed as "chattels" and the federal laws were unclear as to their rights, since they were ostensibly the property of citizens of another nation.

Abolitionists in New England warmed to the Africans' troubles, but first wanted to find out exactly what had happened, and get the Africans' side of the story. Finally, interpreters who could speak their dialect were found and the captured blacks told their woeful tale. They were among many who had been kidnapped in Mendi country, inland in Guinea along the West African coast. Enslaved, they were put on a ship and taken to Cuba. Here the interpreters translate the story of the voyage by one named Grabeau, who was second in command to Cinquez.*

"On board the vessel there was a large number of men, but the women and children were far the most numerous . . . They were fastened together in couples by the wrists and legs, and kept

* Barber, Amistad *Captives.*

in that situation day and night." Grabeau and another of the Africans, named Kimbo, lay down on the floor to show the painful position in which they were obliged to sleep.

"By day it was no better. . . . The space between decks was so small — according to their account not exceeding four feet — that they were obliged, if they attempted to stand to keep in a crouching position. . . . The decks, fore and aft, were crowded to overflowing. . . . They suffered terribly. . . . They had rice enough to eat, but had very little to drink. . . . If they left any of the rice that was given to them uneaten, either from sickness or any other cause, they were whipped. . . . It was a common thing for them to be forced to eat so much as to vomit. . . . Many of the men, women and children died on the passage . . .

"They were landed by night at a small village near Havana. . . . Soon several white men came to buy them, and among them was the one claiming to be their master, whom they called Pipi." Pipi, it turned out, was Don Jose Ruiz, one of the two Spaniards rescued by the Americans on the *Amistad*'s capture. "Pipi, or Ruiz, selected such as he liked and made them stand in a row . . . He then felt of each of them in every part of their body . . . made them open their mouths to see if their teeth were sound . . . and carried the examination to a degree of minuteness of which only a slave dealer would be guilty."

They were separated from their companions who had come with them from Africa, and there was weeping among the women and children, but, Grabeau told the interpreter, he did not weep "because he is a man." Kimbo, who sat by Grabeau during the interview, said he also shed no tears, but he thought of his home in Africa and of friends left there whom he should never see again.

The interpreter continued Grabeau's account: "The men bought by Ruiz were taken on foot through Havana in the night and put on board a vessel." The vessel was the *Amistad*. "During the night they were kept in irons, placed about the hands, feet and neck. . . . They were treated during the day in a somewhat milder manner, though all the irons were never taken off at once. . . . Their allowance of food was very scant, and of water still more so. . . . They were very hungry and suffered much in the hot days and nights from thirst. . . . In addition to this there was much whipping. . . . And the cook told them that when they reached land they would all be eaten. . . . This 'made their hearts burn.' "

The cook's remark was a fatal mistake. It was, of course, heartless teasing on his part. The Spaniards were not cannibals, but the cook, a mulatto, well knew the chord of fear this would strike in the hearts of the slaves. It is probably what made them desperate enough to mutiny.

The captives had been purchased for a cane plantation and were being taken on the *Amistad* to Guanaja, a Cuban port several hundred miles east of Havana. Four days out, Cinquez led the blacks aboard in the uprising. It had stormed during the day and all hands were on deck at work, hauling line and sail to keep the vessel in trim in the high winds. That night all were exhausted and slept, except for the helmsman. The Africans, however, did not sleep. They listened and worked at their chains. At three in the morning, Cinquez and a number of others were free.

Cinquez was described later as a "powerful young rice planter." His father, according to one report, was an African chief. There is little doubt that he was a born leader, his aristocratic coolness under pressure never yielded. An observer of Cinquez while the African was a prisoner in the New Haven jail said "There is something very prepossessing and pleasant in his countenance, and his authority over the others is absolute, but exercised by him with justice and mildness."*

Cinquez was asked how it was possible for the Africans to rise upon the crew when they were chained in the manner described.

* Henry K. Brooke, *Book of Pirates*, Philadelphia, 1841.

[230]

He replied, simply, that the chain which connected the iron collars about their necks was fastened at the end by a padlock, and that this was first broken and afterwards the other irons. Their object in the fray, he insisted to the interpreter, "was to make themselves free."

It is quite possible that without Cinquez, a leader with such force of decision, the mutiny would have not taken place. But the best accounts of the mutiny came from the Spaniards. Joe Ruiz tells his story of the uprising:

"In the night we heard a noise in the forecastle. All of us were asleep except the man at the helm. I do not know how things began. I was awoke by the noise, this man Joseph (Cinquez) I saw. I cannot tell how many were engaged. There was no moon. It was very dark. I took up an oar and tried to quell the mutiny. I cried no! no! I then heard one of the crew cry murder. I then heard the captain order the cabin boy to go below and get some bread to throw to them, in hopes to pacify the Negroes."

To hope that the slaves would drop the mutiny and scramble for food was futile. Antonio testified in court that he had done as ordered but the slaves wouldn't touch the food.

The captain and the cook were slain in the struggle, and their bodies were later tossed overboard. Two of the schooner's sailors escaped by dropping a small boat over the side and fleeing in it.

The second Spaniard, Don Pedro Montez, an older man, gave his account of the mutiny, which, like Ruiz's, was interpreted to the court by a naval officer who spoke Spanish.

"We left Havana on the 28th of June. I owned four slaves, three females and one male. For three days the wind was ahead and all went well. Between 11 and 12 at night, just as the moon was rising, sky dark and cloudy, weather very rainy, on the fourth night I laid down on a mattress. Between three and four I was awakened by a noise which was caused by blows given to the mulatto cook. I went on deck, and they attacked me. I seized

a stick and a knife with a view to defend myself. I did not wish to
kill or hurt them."

Cinquez, Montez said, wounded him on the arm and head with
one of the sugar knives, with which the slaves had armed themselves. Montez said he ran below, stowed himself wrapped in a
sail between two barrels. Cinquez pulled him back on deck where
he and Ruiz were given a choice — navigate the *Amistad* to
Africa or be slain. This was given in words translated by Antonio,
who was also spared in order to communicate with the Spaniards,
and in gestures that left no uncertainty as to their meaning. The
Spaniards accepted the terms — or so the Africans thought.

Cinquez ordered Montez, a former sea captain, to steer for
Africa. But the Africans knew nothing about the sea. None had
seen it before their enslavement, and all they knew was that home
was "two moons" beyond the horizon where the sun rose each
morning.

The Spaniards set out immediately to thwart the plan. By day
they did steer east, toward the sun, but as slowly as possible, tack-
ing back and forth in wide reaches, making as little progress as
possible. On cloudy days, when the slaves couldn't see the sun,
and at night when they alone knew how to navigate by the stars,
the Spaniards headed west and north, hoping to strike land.

Montez told later of the trick. "I steered for Havana in the
night by the stars, but by the sun in the day, taking care to make
no more way than possible. After sailing fifty leagues, we saw
an American merchant ship, but did not speak her. We were also
passed by a schooner but were unnoticed." They boxed back
and forth for days, but contrary to Montez's assumption, the
Amistad was noticed, and reports of the erratic sailing of a
phantom-like "long, low black schooner" which had no obvious
course soon began to appear in Eastern newspapers.

"We kept no reckoning," said Montez. "I did not know how

many days we had been out, nor what day of the week it was when the officers came on board." They stopped at island after island where the Negroes tried to get provisions, sailing away quickly before their presence would draw official attention and possible capture. The Africans feared recapture more than anything else. "We anchored at least thirty times," Montez recounted the adventure. "And lost an anchor at New Providence. When at anchor we were treated well, but at sea they acted very cruelly towards me. They once wanted me to drop anchor in the high seas." No doubt seasick, the Africans were despairing of ever reaching their goal, home and freedom.

For two months the *Amistad* zigzagged across the Atlantic off North America. The Spaniards, assuming they had left the West Indies behind, headed north when they could. Meanwhile, ten of the Africans died en route. Finally, the *Amistad* approached land. The New York harbor boats approached and on seeing and hearing the white men, who were not as swarthy as the Spaniards and spoke nothing like them, Cinquez and the other leaders began to suspect the trickery of the Spaniards. They had, however, no choice but to continue. The *Amistad* proceeded along Long Island until the long, low sandy profile of Montauk Point appeared safe. Cinquez ordered the ship halted while he and others went ashore to get desperately needed water and food. Before they could get back, the men from the *Washington* had seized the *Amistad* and the long flight was ended.

Federal officials began an investigation of the *Amistad* mutiny immediately after the ships reached New London. The legalities of the *Amistad* case rested on the false contention of the Spaniards, who had filed suit to regain the slaves, that the Africans were "ladinoes," or slaves born in Cuba, and not "bozales," blacks taken illegally from Africa after 1820, when Spain had outlawed slave traffic to the New World.

In New Haven the sick were placed in one room, the little girls in another and the rest of the Africans were confined to one large room and once a day were allowed out for exercise.

Cinquez, Grabeau, and several other men waited in quiet, resigned dignity for the death they were certain would come. The American authorities had listened only to the Spaniards' story and now the Africans were imprisoned as the property of Montez and Ruiz.

The abolitionists immediately took note of the pitiful group and formed a committee to raise funds for their legal defense. They entered court on behalf of the Africans and argued that the Africans had come as free persons and should be released to return to their native land.

As noted earlier, the abolitionists had to first learn the Africans' side of the story and considerable difficulties were encountered in getting it. None of the Negroes the abolitionists took to the jail could understand the dialect of the captives. Finally, two Mendis were found on a British warship. When they arrived at the jail, the captives were having breakfast and the jailer objected to the interruption. "One of the captives, however, coming to the door and finding one who could talk his own language, took hold of him and literally dragged him in. Breakfast was forgotten, all seemed overwhelmed with joy, all talking as fast as possible."

Once the Africans' story was made clear, the perfidy of the Spaniards was confirmed. The Africans had been illegally seized and imported into Cuba, violating the laws of Spain. The documents presented by Ruiz and Montez alleging the captives to be ladinoes were marked as frauds. The U.S. District Court ruled that the Africans, being free men at the outset, were still free.

But the case was not finished. The Spaniards and New York business interests with whom they had strange alliances, appealed it to the circuit court. But there the lower court decision was upheld.

The Spanish government had entered the issue and now put considerable pressure on President Martin Van Buren and his administration to release the slaves as property of Spanish citizens. Van Buren's secretary of state and attorney general were Southerners and favored handing over the mutineers. So the government appealed the case to the Supreme Court.

The abolitionists, fearing the heavy odds building up against the handful of Africans they were trying to save, sought out a distinguished defender of liberty to plead their case in the high court. They went to former President John Quincy Adams and persuaded him to enter the legal lists for their cause.

Though a lawyer, Adams had not argued a case in court for more than three decades. He had already expressed much sympathy for the *Amistad* captives but he at first declined to take their case because of his age and ill health. Upon further entreaties, he finally agreed, though still doubting his own strength to see the defense through.

Advocates of slavery could see the *Amistad* case as becoming a precedent of huge importance, threatening their businesses, in fact their whole way of life. When Adams went to Washington he became gravely concerned and sickened at the pressures mounting against the Africans and the obvious efforts to torpedo the case by any means.

Adams wrote that his was "a painful search of means to defeat and expose the abominable conspiracy, executive and judicial, of this government against the lives" of the Africans. Van Buren had been personally embarrassed by the case and the administration wanted the decision overthrown. Thus it became known as the "trial of one president by another."

Adams rose in court and gave one of the most moving appeals

to reason in the history of the high court. He pleaded again and again for "justice," and contended that the Africans were entitled to use the measures they did to protect their freedom which had been usurped. He raged against the Spanish for making the American President serve as a "constable" in the unsavory case. He passionately insisted upon personal liberty for the Africans and called their enslavement "Lilliputian trickery" by Spain.

The Supreme Court upheld the decision. Cinquez and the other captives of the *Amistad* were freed, and another chapter in the fight against slavery came to a close.

AFTERWORD

I HAVE BEEN ASKED WHY I chose to gather these accounts together. What is to be gained by setting before the reader such terrifying histories of such a terrible practice? I can only answer that perhaps these accounts offer a series of windows on a specific point in time, and that in the viewing the reader may acquire some historical perspective on problems presently at hand.

Some years ago I began a casual reading of Atlantic maritime history, and came upon descriptions of the old slave trade. Much was said of the traumatic experience of the slave ship voyage, but there were few eyewitness accounts readily available. There are indeed several excellent and readable histories to be had of the Atlantic slave trade, but the old eyewitness stories have long been out of print.

I share the view of many editors that sometimes the best way to describe something that has happened is to let an individual who took part in it tell about the event in his own words. The first-person story often carries an immediacy and ring of truth that a reader readily perceives despite the sometimes faltering and unpolished delivery of the narrator.

So I began a search for the old eyewitness accounts of the

slave trade and found them in the reference rooms and on the rare-book shelves of the Library of Congress and in several noted Virginia libraries, including the Mariner's Museum Library at Newport News and the Virginia State Library at Richmond. Some of the old works, with the exception of an occasional glance by a scholar looking for source material, had been unused for decades. Others had been reprinted in part forty to eighty years ago, then had disappeared into obscurity.

I am indebted especially for the guidance found in such works as George Dow's *Slavery and Slave Ships*, which has versions of several accounts included here, Evaline Martin's *Journal of a Slave Dealer*, and Elizabeth Donnan's monumental *Documents Illustrative of the History of the Slave Trade to America*.

The passages in the preceding chapters were abstracted with the intention of capsuling as objectively as possible important phases of each writer's experiences. The scope of the offerings has been limited, from the embarkation on the African coast to the landing and sale of the slaves in the New World. This was done for brevity and to focus on the voyage itself. For the voyage was the crucible common to all travelers to the Western Hemisphere. The sufferings and ordeals experienced in the Atlantic voyage westward seemed to mold and change the spirit of those who survived.

Thus the reader, by understanding the aspirations and travails of these ordinary men who lived during what is conceded as one of the blackest eras in mankind's history, may gather something of an insight into the makeup of man today. Man doesn't change as rapidly as the world around him, and the motivations and shortcomings of men living in the latter part of the twentieth century are not much different on analysis than those of one hundred or two hundred years ago.

An acknowledged slave trade does not exist today, of course, but the inhumane treatment of men by other men continues still.

The horrors of World War II concentration camps and death mills rival those of the slave trade and are still very much a part of the memory of millions living now. On lesser scales perhaps, evidences of similar bestialities are reported with frequency from almost all corners of the world.

In reading of this base streak in the character of men, the reader should bear in mind, however, that throughout history there have been groups much like the abolitionists of the eighteenth and nineteenth centuries who fought so doggedly to kill the slave trade and slavery. Where an injustice exists, there eventually will be a set of determined men dedicated to correct it and in so doing project all men to a higher plateau.

BIBLIOGRAPHY

Anonymous, *Liverpool and Slavery, an Historical Account of the Liverpool-African Slave Trade*. Liverpool: A. Bowker & Son, 1884.

Baker, Sir Samuel W., *Ismailia*. New York: Harper, 1875.

Bandinel, James, *Some Account of the Trade in Slaves in Africa as Connected with Europe and America*. London: Longman, Brown, 1842.

Barber, John Warner, *A History of the* Amistad *Captives*. New Haven: E.J. and J.W. Barber, 1840.

Barbot, James, "An Abstract of a Voyage to the New Calabar River, or Rio Real, in the Year 1699." Vol. V, *A Collection of Voyages and Travels*, by Awnsham and John Churchill. London: H. Lintot and J. Osborn, 1744–46.

Blake, W.O., *The History of Slavery and the Slave Trade, Ancient and Modern*. Columbus, Ohio: J. & H. Miller, 1858.

Brooke, Henry K., *The Book of Pirates*. Philadelphia: J.B. Perry, 1841.

Buchanan, Thomas, *Army and Navy Chronicle*. Feb. 13, 1840.

Canot, Theodore, *Captain Canot, or Twenty Years of An African Slaver*. New York: D. Appleton and Co., 1854.

Cecil, Rev. R., *The Works of Rev. John Newton*. London, 1851.

Channing, William E., *The Duty of the Free States*. Glasgow: J. Hedderwick and Sons, 1842.

Churchill, Awnsham and John, *A Collection of Voyages and Travels*. Vols. I–VI. London: H. Lintot and J. Osborn, 1744–46.

Clarkson, Thomas, *An Essay on the Impolicy of the African Trade*. London: J. Phillips, 1788.

———, *History of the Rise, Progress and Accomplishment of the Abolition of the African Slave Trade, by the British Parliament*. London: Longman, Hurst, Rees and Orme, 1808.

Davidson, Basil, *Black Mother, the Years of the African Slave Trade*. Boston: Little, Brown, 1961.

Donnan, Elizabeth, *Documents Illustrative of the History of the Slave Trade to America.* Vols. I–IV. Washington, D.C.: Carnegie Institution of Washington, 1930–35.

Dow, George F., *Slavery and Slave Ships.* Salem, Mass.: Marine Research Society, 1927.

Drake, Richard, *Revelations of a Slave Smuggler, an Autobiography.* New York, 1860.

Edwards, Bryan, *The History, Civil and Commercial, of the British Colonies of the West Indies.* London, 1794.

Equiano, Olaudah, *The Life of Olaudah Equiano, or Gustavus Vassa, the African.* Boston: I. Knapp, 1837.

Falconbridge, Alexander, *An Account of the Slave Trade on the Coast of Africa.* London, 1788.

Foote, Andrew Hull, *Africa and the American Flag.* New York: D. Appleton and Co., 1862.

Hadfield, Robert, L., *Mutiny at Sea.* London: G. Bles, 1938.

Hakluyt, Richard, *The Principal Navigations, Traffiques, Voyages and Discoveries of the English Nation.* London, 1589. Reprinted Edinburgh: E. & G. Goldsmid, 1885–90.

House of Commons, *An Abstract of the Evidence Delivered Before a Select Committee of the House of Commons in the Years 1790 and 1791 for the Abolition of the Slave Trade.* London, 1855.

———, *Debate on the Motion for the Abolition of the Slave Trade.* London, 1792.

House of Lords, *Report on the Abolition of the Slave Trade.* London, 1792.

Howard, Warren S., *American Slavers and the Federal Law.* Berkeley: University of California Press, 1963.

Howe, George, "The Last Slaver," *Scribners Magazine,* July 1890.

Jay, William, *The Creole Case.* New York: New York American, 1842.

Lewis, Matthew Gregory, *The Journal of a West Indian Proprietor.* London: J. Murray, 1834.

Lloyd, Christopher, *The Navy and the Slave Trade.* London, New York: Longmans, Green, 1949.

MacKenzie-Grieve, Averil S., *The Last Years of the English Slave Trade.* London: Putnam & Co. Ltd., 1941.

Manning, Edward, *Six Months on a Slaver.* New York: Harper & Brothers, 1879.

Mannix, Daniel, *Black Cargoes, A History of the Atlantic Slave Trade,* 1518–1865. New York: Viking Press, 1962.

Martin, Bernard, *John Newton, a Biography.* London: Heinemann, 1950.

Miller, Basil W., *Ten Slaves Who Became Famous.* Grand Rapids: Zondervan Publishing House, 1951.

O'Callaghan, Edmund B., *Voyages of the St. John and Arms of Amsterdam.* Albany, N.Y.: J. Munsell, 1867.

O'Callaghan, Sean, *The Slave Trade Today*. New York: Crown Publishers, 1961.

Owen, Nics., *Journal of a Slave Dealer*, edited by Evaline Martin. London: G. Routledge and Sons, Ltd., 1930.

Owens, William A., *Slave Mutiny, The Revolt of the Schooner* Amistad. New York: John Day Co., 1953.

Parliament, Extracts from the Evidence Taken Before Committees of Both Houses of Parliament Relative to the Slave Trade. London, 1851.

Phillips, Thomas, "Journal," Vol. VI, *A Collection of Voyages and Travels*, by Awnsham and John Churchill. London, 1746.

Pinckard, Dr. George, *Notes on the West Indies*. London: Longman, Hurst, Rees and Orme, 1806.

Robbins, Archibald, *A Journal Comprising an Account of the Loss of the Brig* Commerce. Hartford: S. Angus, 1828.

Rockwell, John Arnold, Letter to John M. Clayton, Secretary of State, in relation to the Barque *Jones*. Washington, D.C.: Gideon, 1849.

Rodway, James, *The West Indies and the Spanish Main*. London: T.F. Unwin, 1896.

Rukeyser, Muriel, *Willard Gibbs*. Garden City, N.Y.: Doubleday, Doran & Co., Inc., 1942.

Snelgrave, William, *A New Account of Some Parts of Guinea and the Slave Trade*. London: J., J and P. Knapton, 1734.

Spears, John R., *The American Slave Trade*. London: Bickers & Son, 1900.

Stanfield, James F., *The Guinea Voyage and Letters*. London, 1807.

Stedman, John G., *Narrative of a Five Years' Expedition Against the Revolt in Surinam*. London, 1796.

Swann, Alfred J., *Fighting the Slave Hunters in Central Africa*. Philadelphia: J.B. Lippincott Co., 1910.

Taussig, Charles W., *Rum, Romance and Rebellion*. New York: Minton, Balch & Co., 1928.

Unwin, Rayner, *The Defeat of John Hawkins, a Biography of His Third Slaving Voyage*. New York: Macmillan, 1960.

Wadstrom, Carl Bernhard, *Observations on the Slave Trade*. London: J. Phillips, 1789.

Wiedner, Donald L., *A History of Africa South of the Sahara*. New York: Random House, 1962.

Williams, Gomer, *The Liverpool Privateers*. London: W. Heinemann, 1897.